St Mary Magdalen in Provence

The Coffin and the Cave

Mary and Companions arriving in Provence.

St Mary Magdalen in Provence

The Coffin and the Cave

A Spiritual Travelogue

Michael Donley

'... the indestructible truth of legend ...'
(Patrick Leigh Fermor, **Mani**)

GRACEWING

Gracewing
2 Southern Avenue, Leominster
Herefordshire HR6 0QF

ISBN 978 0 85244 177 0

Reprinted 2014

Typeset by Action Publishing Technology Ltd,
Gloucester GL1 5SR

For my granddaughter
Amélie
who loved books
before she could walk or talk

Contents

Prologue

Early on Friday 26 April in the year 1336 Francesco Petrarch set out with his brother, Gherardo, to climb Mont Ventoux. As its name suggests, it is a windswept mountain rising to almost 2,000 metres, north-east of Avignon. Planning a pre-dawn start, they had spent the night at an auberge in Malaucène, the village that nestles at its foot and which boasts the largest and possibly the oldest plane trees in the whole of Provence.

Petrarch had lived in the area since the age of eight when his father, like Dante, had been expelled from Florence. Carpentras – the town nearest the mountain and the one they had passed through on the way – was where he had spent his boyhood and youth, before becoming attached to the exiled papal court at Avignon. Rising from a low plain, this most westerly peak of the Alps, this *Géant de Provence* is visible from afar in any direction. Petrarch had long dreamed of scaling it. In order, he said, to appreciate the view. At the age of thirty-two, he was about to fulfil his ambition. On a fine spring day such as this, now that the winter cap of snow had melted, the prospect from the summit would not be obscured by winter mist and not yet a prey to summer haze.

There were no recognizable tracks beyond the foothills in 1336, for few if any had ventured up before him. Nowadays, you can reach the top by car. The view remains every bit as grandiose, and may help you turn a blind eye to the observatory, the radar station, the TV masts, the hotel, the ski lifts and – should it be the appropriate day of the year – the circus that follows on the heels of the participants in the Tour de France. For Petrarch it would be a long, arduous climb. Even today, with all the advantages of the *Grandes Randonnées* pathways, a seasoned hiker must nonetheless set aside five hours to get to the top.

At the close of day, as a late supper was being prepared back at the inn in Malaucène, he wasted no time in jotting down his thoughts in what has become the most famous of his six hundred lengthy letters. Written in Latin, like most of his works, it is addressed to Dionigi (Dionysius) da Borgo San Sepolcro – Augustinian monk, theologian and his former confessor. Petrarch tells how he was surprised by the quality of the air on the summit and undeniably impressed by the far-reaching views that extended on all sides over the clouds that clung to the slopes: the Italian Alps, the bay of Marseilles, Aigues Mortes in its Camargue lagoon. Yet in all the dozen or so pages, it is something to which he devotes a mere ten lines.

'To Dionigi,' he had begun, 'concerning some personal problems.' A strange way to introduce an account of a mountain climb!

Yet there is a further peculiarity: the precise manner of his ascent. He describes how, as the way became ever more precarious, the industrious Gherardo opted for a direct if steep path. Petrarch, for his part, decided on a longer but seemingly less arduous route. When his brother had already reached a considerable height, he was still wandering about in the valleys, aware that he had merely succeeded in increasing the distance and the difficulty. Stubbornly, however, he refused to admit defeat and went on to make the same mistake at least three more times, much to Gherardo's amusement.

Resting on the summit, when he finally reached it, Petrarch took out a book that had never left his side since first it had been given to him three years before the climb, given by none other than Dionigi: the *Confessions* of St Augustine. Reading at random, he would have us believe, his eyes fell on the following passage: 'Men will travel to admire high mountains and the mighty waves of the seas, and the rolling rivers and the ring of the oceans and the wheeling of the stars; yet to themselves they give no heed.' He then closed the book, forgetting the external view and directed his gaze inwards. Throughout the descent, under a full moon, he had remained silent.

It is impossible to determine in detail the veracity of this account, the more so since Petrarch was in the habit of collating, editing and even rewriting his own copies of his correspondence. Indeed, the final version of the letter on Mont Ventoux is believed to date from some seventeen years after the event, at a time when Dionigi himself had been dead for ten years. The entire venture has become an allegory, a pilgrim's progress. Yet not in any vague, generalized sense. Petrarch's primary concern was not with Everyman; as the letter specifies, it was his own 'personal problems' that preoccupied him.

The allusion is to the tensions that informed his entire adult life, providing the permanent themes of most of his writings. There was, above all, the unrequited and forbidden love for 'Laura' which still tormented him, as much to his shame as his delight. If indeed she was an actual person, his first glimpse of this married and virtuous lady – a meeting that has become as famous as that between Dante and Beatrice – had taken place, like the ascent of Ventoux, on a Friday in April. There was also the immoderate desire for ever greater worldly fame, the wish to celebrate the authors of classical antiquity with himself as their champion – as against a feeling of guilt at having already achieved a considerable degree of such fame, combined with a growing disdain for the things of this world. There was his increasing disgust at the sinful goings-on at the papal court in Avignon, coupled with feelings of self-criticism for ever having had anything to do with the place. Petrarch may not have been the first to link geographical height with spiritual ascent – the theme is at least as old as Moses, as old as the hills, we might say – yet there is no diminishing his inner anguish as the conviction grows within him that he has strayed from the right path and wasted time wandering self-indulgently in the valleys in search of illusory pleasures.

Gherardo, on the other hand, had proved the more decisive and taken the straight path to salvation. In fact, for years the two brothers had discussed the possibility of his becoming a monk. In 1343, not many years after the ascent of Ventoux and also in the month of April, he entered the Charterhouse of Montrieux, half a day's ride to the southeast.

Given the close relationship the brothers enjoyed, it was an event that caused Petrarch considerable sadness. Not that he disagreed with the decision. On the contrary, it was perhaps his own involvement in the making of it, together with his admiration for Gherardo, that provoked in him the spiritual crisis that was to have such a marked effect on his personality and on his writings, challenging him to make the sort of self-examination he refers to in the Ventoux letter. From then on, he returned time and again to the contrast between Gherardo's choice and his own contradictory efforts. Even the legend of the foundation of Montrieux seemed to hold a message for him. Referring to it in another of his letters, he tells of how one of a pair of brothers, deciding to forsake worldly pleasures, withdrew to this very spot. His example eventually converted the other brother, so that between them they formed the nucleus of what was to become the same monastery that, despite many vicissitudes, is still active today.

Petrarch never did follow Gherardo's example, though he half-longed to do so. For years he had lived in a modest house in the hamlet of Vaucluse – *Vallis clausa*, a 'valley enclosed' – on the south bank of the River Sorgue, a tributary of the Rhône. The house was demolished, whatever the tourist literature might suggest, during his own lifetime. It was not far from an overhanging cliff 230 metres high at whose base is a mysterious grotto. In spring and autumn, emerald green waters surge up from subterranean drainage pockets 90 metres below, in what is the most powerful of such 'fountains' in all France. Even today the population numbers a mere 611 inhabitants. Yet, whether because of its charm or its associations with Petrarch or both, it was the name of this humble settlement – rather than of a river, as was more usual – that was given to the entire *département* during the revolutionary reorganization of 1793. Thereafter the hamlet itself became known as Fontaine-de-Vaucluse.

Petrarch had first visited the area as a boy of twelve when living at Carpentras, and had been transfixed. Even at that age, he had formed the desire to live there one day. It was a place of rural peace, where he mixed studious seclusion – writing or conceiving many of his greatest works – with periods of travel, whether in France or Italy, Flanders or Germany.

As an old man writing from Italy, where he had retired, Petrarch fondly recalls 'the hills and the caves, the woods and the mossy stones amid which winds the Sorgue'. It was a landscape across which he had been in the habit of walking alone, at night under the stars and moon. This preference for the countryside and for relative solitude underlines that strand in his make-up that might have led him to take the path Gherardo had chosen. Instead, he had been half-hearted, meandering – literally and symbolically – in the valley of Vaucluse.

As for Mont Ventoux, there is no evidence that Petrarch ever scaled it a second time. He did climb another mountain range – though this is less well known – on at least three occasions: the Massif de la Sainte-Baume. From the summit of Ventoux on that April day in 1336, it would have been one of the geographical features that presented itself, beyond and higher than both the Lubéron and Cézanne's Sainte-Victoire. Whether or not Petrarch noticed it is another matter. Yet, conversely, when he first visited it – just one year later – he may well have spotted the tip of Mont Ventoux and remembered the recent expedition made there in the company of Gherardo. Moreover, the very rewriting of the letter detailing that earlier ascent may perhaps have been influenced by his visits to this other range, the Sainte-Baume.

Why might this be so?

High up in this more southerly range is a vast cave. The very cave in which Gherardo finally decided that he would indeed enter the Charterhouse of Montrieux, itself but a mere twenty kilometres distant.

❧

Mont Rieux – as it would have been written in Petrarch's time – had for a century or so been a Benedictine house, although its history is thought to go back even further still. Since becoming a Carthusian establishment in the early twelfth century, it has survived a number of difficulties. Of the thirty-five monks resident when the Black Death struck in 1348 only one seems to have survived – Gherardo himself. In fact, it was Petrarch who used his influence in Italy, where he was then living, to see that funds were made available for the reinvigoration of the establishment. Pillaged on more than one occasion in the sixteenth century, it also suffered damage in 1707 at the hands of Austrian troops during the War of the Spanish Succession. Following the upheavals occasioned by the Revolution, it was sold off in 1792. It was bought back and restored in 1843 only to be confiscated in 1901, at a time when anticlericalism was gaining the upper hand in French politics. Phoenix-like it reopened again in 1928. Though not totally immune from hostilities during the Second World War, it was felt to be a safe enough spot to serve as refuge for a maternity clinic from Toulon. Never must the crying of newborn babies have sounded more incongruous than in this *Zone de Silence*. To the present day it has managed to maintain an austere, enclosed lifestyle after the pattern set by the founder of the Carthusians, St Bruno.

Over the centuries benefactors enabled the monks to surround themselves with ever more acres of ilex and cork-oaks, thus creating their own 'desert'. The buildings themselves are set in a valley which is fertile, if isolated. Through the valley flows a river, the Gapeau. It is, Petrarch might have said, a more authentic version of his own Vaucluse.

Some two and a half hours' walk away is the curiously weathered dolomite formation known as Les Aiguilles (or Needles) de Valbelle, sometimes described as a 'cité dolomitique' because the rocks – spread over a vast area – are shaped like houses, mansions and castles. They are named after the Comte de Valbelle, Louis XV's Lieutenant de Provence. As for the name Montrieux, this derives ultimately from the Latin *Mons Rivulorum*, for these hillsides are rich in streams and springs. In Provençal this became *Mount dei riou* or *Montdriou*, hence the current appellation.

Public access is forbidden even today, except to a specially provided chapel and a small shop where honey and other monastic products are sold. Petrarch, however, was able to visit on several occasions, most famously in the winter of 1347, four years after Gherardo had taken his vows. He was a welcome guest, fêted as befitted someone who had been publicly crowned with a laurel wreath in the Capitol at Rome as foremost poet and scholar of his age, the first poet laureate of modern times. He was nonetheless unwilling to disturb the rigid discipline of the monks for more than a day and a night. As his stay drew to its close, the Prior and the brothers accompanied him through the forest paths to the limits of their territory – such a group walk, once a week, being their only recreation and conversation. His sadness at leaving was undoubtedly tempered by his setting to work, during Lent of that year, on a book in which he expressed at length what he was not able to say in person.

Dedicated to Gherardo, the *De Otio Religioso* is a lengthy paean to the stillness, recollection and asceticism of the monastic way of life. It is perhaps the most emphatic of his many texts on religious themes among which are *De Vita Solitaria*; a sequence of *Penitential Psalms*; and the

Secretum or 'Petrarch's Secret', in which he converses with St Augustine on the path he has taken in life, in the process laying his soul bare to an extent that no European since Augustine, in fact, had done.

Even the *Canzoniere* – the sonnet sequence inspired by Laura and written in Italian (exceptionally for this master of Latin prose) – for which Petrarch has posthumously become so narrowly famous are hardly an attempt to immortalize her in verse, in the manner of Ronsard's *Sonnets pour Hélène.* Nor are they a reworking of Horace's *carpe diem* theme. Like the texts referred to above, they too are essentially a penitential comment on the vanity and transience of worldly desire.

Another of his writings – the *Bucolicum Carmen* – is a series of pastoral eclogues modelled on Virgil. Yet here too the religious theme appears. The first of these eclogues describes a certain Silvanus and Monicus. As Petrarch makes clear in one of his letters to Gherardo, Silvanus represents Petrarch himself. (This was, it seems, a nickname given him on account of his love of forests as opposed to towns and cities.) Monicus, on the other hand, stands for Gherardo. He then adds an interesting note of explanation concerning the dwelling place of this monk. 'The cave where Monicus lives in solitude is Montrieux where you now lead a monastic life [...] or else that grotto near your monastery where Mary Magdalen lived as a penitent.'

Mary Magdalen?

It is understandable that she be mentioned in *De Otio Religioso*, as a role model, a person 'changed from a citizen of Babylon into a citizen of the heavenly Jerusalem'. But dwelling in a Provençal cave? 'Near your monastery...' To which place is Petrarch referring? The same cave in the Massif de la Sainte-Baume with which he was himself familiar and in which Gherardo had finally resolved to take monastic vows.

Even in their day it had for centuries been a place of pilgrimage as the spot according to ancient tradition where Mary Magdalen had ended her days as an anchorite. It was certainly an appropriate place in which Gherardo should have decided that he too would become, if not a hermit, then a member of a strict, enclosed order. Indeed, the monastery's own archives indicate that – despite the legend of the two brothers referred to above – it owes its very existence to the proximity of the cave. It seems its original benefactor had been a wealthy Italian. Suffering from a grave illness, in 1117 he arranged to be transported on pilgrimage to the Sainte-Baume in order to seek the intercession of Mary Magdalen. If healed, he vowed he would found a Charterhouse in the vicinity. The Carthusian order had only relatively recently been founded (1054). Miraculously cured, he was true to his word, selling all his possessions and eventually taking the habit himself.

Petrarch refers to his own visits to this cave in several of his writings. It was, after all, on his route when visiting his brother at Montrieux. His first visit, in 1337, the year after the ascent of Mont Ventoux, had been to accompany an important personage at the request of Cardinal Colonna of Avignon. He had stayed three days and nights, 'non sine volupte', not without pleasure. It was during this visit that he composed a poem consisting of thirty-six Latin hexameters in honour of the saint and the Provençal tradition concerning her. It was a youthful composition which he had all but forgotten until in 1369, some thirty-five years later, one of his oldest and dearest friends – Philippe de Cabassole, Bishop of Cavaillon (in whose diocese Vaucluse was situated) – wrote to Italy reminding him of it, and requesting a copy. Philippe himself had a special devotion to Mary Magdalen and had even written a book about her. 'I did it extemporaneously and rapidly,' Petrarch notes in his reply,

> because of my enthusiasm and youthful daring. [. . .] Upon my return, I read to you the unrevised verses which had been written in your name and mine, inasmuch as I had composed them with you as an imaginary witness and prompter [and now] with a certain pleasure you may recall the first essays of my youth.

Apparently a copy was painted onto a tablet which was then displayed in the grotto. With the ravages of time and the humidity of the place, the letters inevitably became difficult to decipher. However, various efforts to restore or replace the inscription have taken place over the centuries. The latest version – engraved on a marble plaque on the right as you enter – dates from 1955 and is by courtesy of a Franco-Italian cultural association. You might otherwise never learn of the poem's existence, for it never seems to feature in Petrarchan anthologies (unlike the letter describing the ascent of Ventoux) and fails to attract the attention of those specialists who see in Petrarch only the Father of Humanism or writer of Italian love sonnets. For this reason alone, it is worth reproducing. It might be freely translated as follows:

Dear friend of God, be moved by our tears;
Hearken to my prayers and consider our salvation,
As indeed thou canst. For not in vain wast thou permitted
To touch and wash with thy tears those holy feet,
To dry them with thy shining hair and kiss them,
And on the Lord's head sprinkle precious perfumes.
Nor in vain, when He rose up from the dead,
Did Christ, King of heavenly Olympus,
Meet thee first, vouchsafing thee to hear His voice
And see His limbs in their
Immortal glory and eternal splendour.
He had seen thee stay close by His cross,
Unafraid of dire torments at Jewish hands
Or of the jibes and insults of the furious mob,
Their tongues cruel as the scourge.
But, sorrowful yet brave,
Thou didst run thy fingers o'er the gory nails,
Thy tears drenching His wounds, thy savage fists
Beating thy fair breast, thy hands relentlessly
Tearing at thy golden hair. This, I say, He saw
As His erstwhile trusty men
Scattered, their valour deserting them.
Mindful of it, He appeared first to thee ere any other,
To thee alone presented first Himself.

Then, leaving earth and to the heavens returning,
He nourished thee for thirty years beneath this cliff.
Ne'er needing mortal food for so long a time, thou wast
Content with naught but divine nourishment and wholesome dew.
This cave, damp from the dripping rocks and
Gloomy with horrid slime, was yet to thee a home
Excelling the golden palaces of kings,
The richest of domains and every pleasure.
Here willingly confined, clothed in naught but thy long hair,
'Tis said thou didst endure thrice ten Decembers,
Not weakened by the frost nor cowed by dread,
Since hunger, cold, and the hard bed of stone
Were sweetened by the love and hope deep-seated in thy breast.
Here unseen by human eye, surrounded by angelic hosts,
Seven times a day for the canonical hours
Wast thou from thy bodily prison
Transported, and to hear the choirs of heaven in antiphonal chant
Found worthy.

It is a poem in which Petrarch has managed to include most of the legends that have attached themselves to the tradition. However, he makes no reference – perhaps for reasons of cohesion – to the equally strong tradition that Mary's coffin lies in the crypt of the vast new basilica whose construction had been started some fifty years previously, precisely because of this tradition, in the town at the northern foot of the mountain: Saint-Maximin-la-Sainte-Baume. We know from his letters that he passed through the place on his way to visit Gherardo. To pay one's respects in this crypt before climbing to the cave had already for generations been part and parcel of the same pilgrimage, as indeed it still is. It seems probable, then, that on at least one occasion the two brothers will have venerated the coffin.

Could it really be that of Mary Magdalen? And the cave? Certainly, despite the secondary accretions that always attach themselves to such traditions, Provençal memory stubbornly and with relative sobriety insists on connecting her with its heartland.

In recent years, many speculative theories about this beguiling figure have found their way into print. Yet the ancient legends of the coffin and the cave – once the focus of pilgrims throughout Christendom – are today, in the English-speaking world, largely unknown. So let us follow in the footsteps of Petrarch. Not in search of some will-o'-the-wisp Laura, but Mary of Magdala herself.

When the limpet legends have been scraped away, will we find within the tradition a kernel of truth?

Part One

The Cave

1

La Sainte-Baume

Rising to some 1150 metres, the Massif or Chaîne de la Sainte-Baume is the highest mountain range in southern Provence. As the crow flies, it is some twenty kilometres from the waters of the Mediterranean and thirty east of Marseilles. Its ridge runs for twelve kilometres in an east–westerly direction, straddling the *départements* of the Var and the Bouches-du-Rhône. In the setting sun this limestone mass belies its craggy solidity, glowing softly like pink marshmallow.

It presents two very different facets: the *adret* and the *ubac*. These two words – which you will find here and there, with slight variations in spelling, on any detailed map of Provence – refer respectively to the southern and northern aspects of a hill or mountain. The *adret* of the Sainte-Baume is bare, arid, gleaming white like the skeleton of a giant corpse picked clean by a thousand vultures. It is the sort of landscape, photographed from the air, that opens the film version of Pagnol's *La Gloire de mon Père*. Indeed, the *Garlaban* – mentioned by name in Pagnol's text – is its westward outcrop. All is as you would expect: typically Provençal.

Not so the *ubac*. Ascending the northern slopes from Nans-les-Pins, you soon realize why this section, with its steeply rising twists and hairpin bends, is the scene of an annual car rally in April or May. Eventually you reach the long, wide shelf-like plateau of Plan d'Aups, spread before you at a cool 700 metres as smooth as a tablecloth. Over on its far side you are confronted by the ridge itself, rising majestically like a stone curtain for another 300 metres. If, wishing to go higher still, you were not obliged to abandon your vehicle at this point, you would stop anyway, in awe of this natural backcloth.

It is a paradise for rock climbers and walkers, but not without its dangers. Mists and fierce winds can suddenly besiege the ridge, even in this seemingly benign part of France. Snow can linger for more than a month, even below the summit. On clear summer days, danger still lurks; for potholes and crevices, as well as the often slippery and crumbly rocks, have between them claimed more than one human victim. Wild boar too, despite being presumably more at home in these surroundings, have been known to lose their footing and fall to their deaths.

Taking your bearings as you close the door of your car, you become aware of a complex of buildings: the Hôtellerie, an Écomusée (formerly a Maison de Retraite called Nazareth) and a bar-restaurant. None is older than the mid-nineteenth century, when pilgrimages were actively promoted again, after the ravages of the Revolution. Despite their sprawling size and extent, they seem lost. Not just on account of the ridge towering behind them to your right, nor simply because of the seeming endlessness of the level ground that stretches before you like a runway. It is as much a result of the infinity of blue to your left, the rest of Provence having disappeared over the edge of the plateau.

As well as pilgrims, you will come across groups of scouts, ramblers, long-distance walkers, visitors to the Ecological Museum or people who have simply come up for the air. The museum's programme of activities covers all things Provençal: language, literature, music, song, dance and theatre. More localized subjects, too: the flora and fauna of the Sainte-Baume; accounts of the earliest human habitation (some 130,000 years BC); mushroom days; the life and work of the old charcoal burners. Or of the ice merchants; for more than one spot on this northern side of the range is called *La Glacière* or *Les Glacières*. Some of these natural iceboxes are twenty metres deep. Vast shallow basins were scooped out nearby and, on winter evenings, filled with water from the many springs. The ice was collected the following morning and preserved for sale during the hotter months in Brignoles, Aubagne, Aix, Toulon and Marseilles. The last wagon pulled up in Marseilles' *Rue de la Glace* in 1928.

In the shade of the curtain of rock, protected from the southern winds and sun, benefitting from the cool and the humidity, there flourishes an ancient deciduous forest that is unique in these latitudes. This *forêt relique* is all that remains of a vast carpet of trees that covered most of Provence at the close of the Tertiary Era. From a distance the expanse of tightly packed tree tops resembles a dark green wave that curls up the foot of the cliff, frozen in mid lap. Since the Victorians, we have grown used to the construction of hothouses in which southern species are enabled to survive in northern climes. Here, the opposite phenomenon is in evidence. In this microclimate, Provence seems to vanish with each step.

The plateau itself, in the stickiest of Provençal summers, is invitingly fresh. The forest all the more so. There are many places which even the penetrating light of the Midi is unable ever to reach. As you begin the final, hour-long ascent to the cave, you set foot in some 350 acres of broad-leaved trees – beeches, limes, sycamores, maples and majestic oaks – together with holly, yews, privets. Most grow to imposing heights, for this forest is protected, *hors coupe*. No tree is ever felled, nor any branch lopped, unless already dead. Gone are the olive trees, the ilex, the fragrant Aleppo, the parasol pines, the sparse *garrigue*. Even the cork-oaks so typical of the region can make it no further than the plateau. You have left them behind with your car. A line could be drawn where the vegetation and flora change. The shrill insistence of the cicadas gradually fades into nothingness. Yet, shady and silent though this forest may be, it conveys no feeling of unease.

Ferns, moss and non-Mediterranean species of flowers

proliferate. Everywhere water trickles and seeps, or perhaps gushes. For this range is the main water tower of Provence; it is from here that all its rivers begin their journey – the Huveaune, the Caramy, the Gapeau, and the Argens. As Lacordaire put it, writing in the nineteenth century, this is undeniably the soil and sky of the Midi, but supporting the vegetation one would expect to find in the mighty forests of medieval England.

How many of those who nowadays come to this part of 'la Provence verte' in search of pastis-and-pétanque relaxation have any idea of the number of high-ranking dignitaries and celebrated persons who, like Petrarch, have climbed up through this forest as humble pilgrims? Kings and queens, popes and cardinals, saints and sinners. Not for nothing is the route up from Nans-les-Pins known as the Chemin des Rois. Until it was destroyed by the revolutionaries in 1793, a *Journalier* (a Register or Visitors' Book) was kept by the monks at the cave. Luckily, details have survived in Pierre-Joseph de Haitze's *Histoire d'Aix*. Haitze, who was born in Cavaillon but lived in Aix, was a prolific researcher; his six-volume *Histoire*, left in manuscript form on his death in 1736, was published in the late nineteenth century.

These ancient trees – some of them a thousand years old – must have witnessed many a spectacle.

In 816 Pope Stephen IV set out from Rome for Rheims. He was to crown, as Emperor, Louis the Pious, son of Charlemagne. He took time out, however, to make the climb. He was followed in 878 by Pope John VIII, on his way to crown another king. Some two years later came Boso I, King of Provence. (The region was not yet part of France.) William the Liberator, Count of Provence and Boso's son – subsequent to his success in liberating Provence from the Saracens around 972 – came to offer thanks.

In the summer of 1254, Louis IX disembarked at Hyères on his return from the Holy Land. This monarch, the future St Louis – who some ten years earlier had commissioned the building of that masterpiece of Gothic architecture, the Sainte Chapelle in Paris – did not fail to come and pray (on 22 July, Mary Magdalen's feast day) in these very different surroundings.

In the 1300s a succession of popes made the climb: in 1309 Clement V – the first to reside in Avignon, given the difficulties Rome was experiencing; John XXII in 1316; Clement VI in 1345; Urban V in 1362.

A single day in 1332 saw the visit of no less than five kings: Philip VI of France, whose reign was dominated by the Hundred Years' War with England; Alphonse IV of Aragon; Hugh IV of Cyprus; John of Luxembourg, King of Bohemia (killed by the English fourteen years later at Crécy); and Robert of Anjou, Count of Provence, King of Naples and titular King of Jerusalem and Sicily. It was this same Robert whom Petrarch had to visit in Naples in 1341, after accepting the offer of the Roman Senate to crown him poet laureate. On that occasion King Robert – a promoter of the new learning – wished first to engage Petrarch in what amounted to an oral examination. As for the grotto, Robert's interest is further shown by the fact that he had protective grilles erected inside the cave, around the dry part of the rock on which Mary Magdalen is said to have rested.

In 1340, together with her husband and children, Bridget of Sweden made the pilgrimage. Some six years later, after the death of her husband, she herself became a nun and founded her own order. She would later be canonized, as would one of her daughters, Catherine.

In 1348 it was the turn of a very different lady: Queen Jeanne. Jeanne was the beautiful and amorous daughter of Robert. She was also his successor, and thus Queen of Naples, Countess of Provence and titular Queen of Sicily and Jerusalem. In Naples, her reputation as a monarch was not good. In Provence, on the other hand, places named after her abound: châteaux, chapels, palaces, gardens, streets ... It seems not to have mattered that it was she who sold Avignon to the papacy in order to finance the defence of her possessions against Louis of Hungary, brother of her first husband, whom she was accused of murdering. Nor does the fact that she only visited Provence once. Indeed, her very distance seems only to have increased the power of her mythical beauty. Frédéric Mistral, celebrated poet of Provence, likened her place in the affection of the locals to that of Mary Queen of Scots in Scotland. It is striking, then, that on her one visit to the region this four-times married queen – who was, as one source puts it, 'partial to the pleasures of love' – did not fail to climb to the cave where, so she would have believed, a penitent prostitute had spent the last years of her life. What thoughts were in her mind, one wonders, as she entered the cave?

In 1376 St Catherine of Siena came on pilgrimage, en route to Avignon where she intended to persuade Pope Gregory XI to return to Rome. She was successful. In the same year, as he made his way back to the Eternal City, Gregory himself ascended the Sainte-Baume.

Among other visitors over the next hundred years were John II the Good, King of France (1362); Charles IV of Luxembourg, King of Bohemia and German Emperor, founder of the University of Prague and correspondent of Petrarch (1367); Charles VI the Mad, King of France together with Louis II, King of Sicily and Count of Provence (1389); anti-Pope Benedict XIII, driven from Avignon (1405); Queen Yolanda of Aragon, Queen of Louis II, who endowed an annual gift of 200 florins (1409); her son Louis III of Anjou (1430); Isabelle of Lorraine, wife of King René (1435); and in 1438 King René himself, who stayed for a retreat lasting nine days.

1440 saw the visit of Charles VII and his queen, Marie of Anjou, sister of René. It was with Charles that the 17-year-old Jeanne d'Arc had demanded an audience in 1429, insisting that he be crowned as the rightful heir to the French throne. It was he who had granted her an army with which to liberate Orleans and Rheims. Very shortly after the departure of the royal couple a fire broke out in the grotto, destroying the buildings. King René came again in 1442 as did the Dauphin Louis. When Louis returned in 1456 (as Louis XI King of France with his queen, Charlotte of Savoy), he granted a considerable sum of money for the refurbishment of the grotto, even designing the cupola over the altar. He also donated statues of himself and his queen, to be put near the main altar in thanks for the birth of their son (the future Charles VIII). King René returned in 1470, after being widowed, with his second wife Jeanne de Laval.

On 11 December 1481, Provence became part of the Kingdom of France. Thereafter every monarch felt it a point of honour to visit the grotto. Anne of Brittany came in 1499 and paid for the repair of the reliquary. In 1516, when François I came with his queen and his mother – to give thanks on his return from the successful battle of Marignan against the Swiss, fought near Milan – he was upset by the condition of the place, despite the improvements made since the fire. This Renaissance monarch – patron of arts and letters, founder of the Collège de France – granted funds for its restoration. He also commissioned for the entrance to the cave the so-called 'Portail Francois I' (still to be seen, but now down in the Hôtellerie) and had three royal chambers built by the grotto. It was in the same year that Jean Ferrier, Archbishop of Arles and Aix-en-Provence, had seven oratories erected along the Chemin des Rois. Francis returned in 1533 on the occasion of the marriage at Marseilles of his second son (Henry of Orleans) to Catherine de Medici. He was back again in 1538, after the liberation of Provence with a cortège of princesses, and 1500 horse. On 25 October 1564, Catherine de Medici came with her two teenage sons (Charles IX of France and the future Henri II), along with Henri de Navarre (aged 11) – the future Henri IV.

In 1586 and again in 1592, during the Wars of Religion, the grotto was ransacked – the second time despite the fact that a drawbridge had been erected.

After two years as a slave in Tunis, the future St Vincent de Paul – tireless worker for the sick and poor and founder of the first order of non-cloistered nuns devoted to their welfare – managed to escape to Avignon in 1607. He, too, came to the grotto, no doubt to give thanks.

On the 6 March 1622, Louis XIII came on pilgrimage with his wife Anne of Austria, who for long had been unable to conceive. He was accompanied by his entire court, his Scots guard and two Swiss regiments. Prayers were said and indeed a son was born, Louis Dieudonné or Gift of God. In his turn this son, now aged 22 and better known as Louis XIV or the Sun King, himself came on pilgrimage on 5 February 1660. With him came his mother, Cardinal Mazarin (Prime Minister and Tutor) as well as sixty carriages, fifty chariots and 500 mounted guard.

Louis XIV was the last king to pay his respects, although all classes of society continued to make the climb until the Revolution. In 1793 the monastic buildings and the interior of the cave were vandalized; any religious furnishings destroyed – with the exception of one seventeenth-century statue (still there on the left as you enter), which eight stalwarts from the nearby village of Plan d'Aups managed to rescue. It is still possible to make out in the rock face several charred holes, presumably where supports for the framework of the structure were embedded.

As soon as the days of the Terror subsided, reconstruction began. In 1822 the Prefect of Toulon restored the site to its former use as a place of pilgrimage and worship. A lengthy eye-witness account survives of the reconsecration of the cave by the Archbishop of Aix assisted by many clergy on 27 May, the Monday of Pentecost, still now a day of pilgrimage. It was written by the former Vicar-General for the Var to his successor. He describes how, having set off from Nans just after midnight, he was surprised to see that vast crowds had been sleeping out under the trees on the plain. From daybreak, hymns and songs were sung. Sprigs of yew were sported in caps and buttonholes – the sign of a Sainte-Baume pilgrim. (Given the strict laws protecting the forest, this practice wouldn't be allowed now!) Forty to forty-five thousand people were estimated to have attended. Although no officers of the law were present, all was orderly and peaceful. The statue from Plan d'Aups had been returned from its place of safe-keeping; other sculptures had come from Gherardo's Chartreuse de Montrieux.

The next upturn in the sanctuary's fortunes came in 1848, after Lacordaire had paid a visit. In 1851, with his typical energy, this gifted preacher – renowned for the post-revolutionary Notre Dame homilies to which the intelligentsia of Paris flocked – set about reviving the pilgrimages on a regular basis. His aim was not simply to recapture the pre-Revolutionary past; nor simply to complete his life's task of restoring the Dominican Order (banished in 1790) – an Order of which Mary Magdalen was second patron. More importantly, he saw the story of Mary as conveying in graphic manner the very essence of the Gospel: the primacy and power of love, divine and human. He it was who built the Hôtellerie we still see, but down on the plateau now and considerably larger than the one that had clung to the rock by the mouth of the cave. Success was assured. When that indefatigable Victorian travel writer Augustus Hare visited the place in the 1880s (see his *South-Eastern France* of 1890), he noted that on the saint's feast day 10,000 pilgrims regularly made their way up.

And so, although the Sainte-Baume has been overshadowed by other sites, pilgrims have continued to come here down to our own days. Some to remain anonymous, others to become widely known. Among them was Father Charles de Foucauld, modern-day desert dweller. At the major turning points in his life, this saintly ascetic, who lived and died among the Touareg in the Sahara, came here to pray to Mary Magdalen, as his ex-votos testify.

❦

And now here am I, following in this long roll-call of honourable footsteps. Well, not quite. Not today. For the *Chemin des Rois*, which most pilgrims take, is the easiest route and so also the busiest. Small fleur-de-lys mark the way. More as badges of honour than signs, for there is little danger of straying. The path is wide and smooth – suitable for the entourages of the distinguished visitors of yore. Suitable also for the 4x4 used by the handful of Dominicans who live in the small monastery by the mouth of the cave.

The *Chemin des Rois* is the route you naturally choose on your first ascent. Or on the occasion of a festive procession – like yesterday, 22 July, Mary Magdalen's own day. Then there had been four or five hundred of us – bishops, assorted clergy, dozens of teenagers, and several toddlers, some of whom decided to remain in their pushchairs. Babies strapped to backs. A couple of dogs, too.

Today, however, I am back to one of the more secret routes. The *Chemin du Canapé*, so called because halfway up you come across an enormous flat block of rock lying incongruously by the side of the track. Black and mossy, it resembles a *canapé* – in the sense, not of an open sandwich but a couch or divan. No doubt this was the path used by the group of Trappist monks who, for almost a decade, established a community on the plateau shortly after the Revolution, before Lacordaire's efforts. The ground underfoot is natural, the atmosphere more mystical – more suitable for meditation, or simply silent attentiveness. You are far less likely to meet other humans here. There is more birdsong, too. Even on this July morning when the temperature down below has already topped thirty degrees, the chirruping in this exceptional vegetation – if you close your eyes – would suggest an April day in England. Most importantly of all, you have more chance of becoming attuned to the spirit of the forest itself. I have been hearing about this from Philippe.

Philippe Devoucoux du Buysson, Dominican friar who entered the Couvent Royal at Saint-Maximin in 1955 at the age of twenty, later becoming a worker-priest – driving a lorry, working as a goatherd – before serving as *gardien* of the grotto for fifteen years, from 1985. He hadn't thought much about the tradition then. It was at the grotto that he got to know Mary Magdalen. Retired now, he lives down at

Nans-les-Pins, on the edge of the forest, near the very start of the old *Chemin des Rois*. In the 'Maison de Marie Magdeleine' [sic], which is also the headquarters of the 'Fraternité Marie Madeleine'. It is a centre of welcome, information, documentation and research. Here Frère Philippe has assembled some 5,000 books on the subject, and fifty or so videos. As well as a regular newsletter, he has produced some twenty monographs. Yet he is no desk-bound aesthete. His feet are firmly on the ground.

'You know,' he told me during my first visit, 'the *gardien* of the grotto must expect to receive all kinds of people, of all kinds of beliefs and none. When I first took up my post, I used to be puzzled by some of these visitors. These were the ones in search of what they called the site's "energies".'

He stretched his mouth sideways on this last word, pulling it out of shape. 'I was sceptical,' he continued. 'But I was wrong!'

As he paused, his face slowly relaxed into an infectious smile. 'Actually, I'm a very early riser. I'm usually in the forest by 6 a.m. At that hour, as the first rays of the sun touch the trees, you can't fail to feel all around you the energy surging up from deep in the ground as the sap rises. Some of the trees are two metres in circumference. The amount needed is enormous! Can you imagine? ... You can't fail to feel something ... It's scientifically undeniable!'

He paused again, as if reliving the experience.

'Actually, whether Mary Magdalen came here or not, the forest hasn't changed much since her day. These trees ... some of the ones you see today are a thousand years old! I'm sure they look down at us as we walk through the forest and chuckle among themselves. At us newcomers ... Compared to them, we're just comical upstarts! We think we're so important because ... because we have mobile phones ... and the internet. Well, they've got something better than that! They've heard the conversations of St Louis, of François the First, and the Sun King himself!'

Like his beloved trees, Philippe chuckled.

Fancying that some 'prim and proper' Christians might

suspect him of being a pantheist, I asked whether he had ever had to rebut this charge.

'*Mon Dieu*! What stupidity!' he said, nodding.

He laughed out loud. We both did. He had not heard the word before, but agreed with me when I suggested that he was, on the contrary, that profoundly orthodox thing, a 'pan-en-theist'.

'Well, yes!' he replied. 'Like St Paul, when he preached in Athens.'

I smiled, for he was referring to the very chapter from the Acts of the Apostles that I myself had in mind: 'In [God] – *en theo* – we live and move and have our being' (17:28). It is a perspective which encompasses the whole (*pan*) of creation, including Philip's trees. The entire cosmos, in fact. One vast Burning Bush, every inch of it hallowed ground, had we but eyes to see.

❧

I had seen horse droppings in the forest and, changing the subject, enquired as to who might be allowed to ride there.

'Oh, that would be the *garde forestier*,' Philippe replied. 'He loves this place, too. Actually, he's told the *Office National des Forêts* quite bluntly that he has no intention of being moved, even if it means sacrificing all chance of promotion. You know, when he shows groups of children round, he doesn't waste time indulging in scientific classification. "This is an oak ... that's a yew ..." and so on. No, he gets them to touch, to smell, to put their arms round the trees as far as their little arms will stretch. To hug, to embrace. He has the right approach.'

I had shown Philippe the small pamphlet picked up on a visit to the Écomusée: *Promenades dans la Montagne Sacrée*. He agreed that the area was indeed sacred, in the widest sense. All the necessary elements are present: Mountain (a geologically rare one, the more ancient layers having risen to cover the more recent ones), untouched Forest, Springs and Grotto.

In this karstic range – whose East–West alignment follows the course of the sun – with its subterranean reserves of water, the Speleological Club of Marseilles has listed twenty springs and 180 sizeable cavities, chasms and potholes. This in addition to the larger caverns, such as the Grotte des Cèdres, the Grotte aux Œufs and the Grotte de Sainte Marie-Madeleine itself, the largest and the most sacred. The steps that lead the present-day visitor to its very mouth are barely a century old. Before the fifth century, when the first monks came, there were no steps at all. In those days it must have been difficult to get to, dark and mysterious, penetrating deep into the womb of the earth.

The place is one of the oldest known sites in the west for the worship of virgin-mother goddesses with their twin powers of life and death. When the city of Marseilles was founded in 600 BC by Greeks from Phocaea (the modern-day Turkish Foça) near Ephesus (Izmir) in Asia Minor, they brought with them their devotion to Artemis, also known as Diana. Unlike in mainland Greece, in Ephesus she had become identified with Cybele and was thought of primarily as a fertility goddess and, interestingly, goddess of caverns, among other things. She was still being worshipped there, where her celebrated temple stood, in New Testament times – one of the Seven Wonders of the Ancient World. The account of the silversmiths' riot given in the Acts of the Apostles makes this clear. It seems that a certain silversmith called Demetrius, who employed a large number of craftsmen making silver shrines of Diana, called a meeting of his men along with others in the same trade. He urged them to speak out against Paul, whose preaching he saw as posing a threat to the Temple's importance and to his own livelihood. This man, he argued, was trying to take away the prestige of a goddess who, as he says, 'is worshipped all over Asia'. Roused to fury by his speech, they started to shout, 'Great is Diana of the Ephesians!'

A statue of her, with her multitude of breasts, can be seen in Marseilles' *Musée d'Archéologie Méditerranéenne.*

It cannot be over-emphasized that Marseilles was a Greek city and remained so culturally long after the general Romanization of the area. In Marseilles the Phocaeans built their own version of the temple at Ephesus and would have copied the Ligurians and Celts in taking the ancient route up the Huveaune valley to the sacred forest and cave, which they would associate with their own Diana.

It was in this connection that Philippe alerted me to a particular passage in the *Pharsalia* – otherwise known as *The [Roman] Civil War* – by the poet Lucan. Writing in the 60s AD, a hundred years after the events, Marcus Annaeus Lucanus recounts Caesar's struggle with Pompey. It is the chapter devoted to Caesar's siege of Massalia (Marseilles) that is of interest. The city had angered him by siding with Pompey. In 49 BC the all-conquering hero is nonetheless stopped in his tracks for six months by the stubborn resistance he encounters. His pride hurt, he decides to cut the town off from the land by constructing a mighty ditch and rampart. The effort required for this – as well as for the necessary siege-works – would be enormous, the amount of timber huge. Local supplies were soon exhausted. It was perhaps, says Philippe, to the Sainte-Baume that he then went. Certainly, anyone familiar with that forest will recognize it in the following lines, given here in Sir Edward Ridley's 1896 translation:

> There stood a sacred grove
> Which from the earliest time no hand of man
> Had dared to violate; hidden from the sun
> Its chill recesses; matted boughs entwined
> Prisoned the air within. [...]
> Still the air, unmoving, yet the leaves
> Filled with mysterious trembling; dripped the streams
> From coal-black fountains. [...]
> Spared in the former war, still dense it rose
> Where all the hills were bare, and Caesar now
> Its fall commanded. But the brawny arms
> Which swayed the axes trembled, and the men,
> Awed by the sacred grove's dark majesty,

Held back the blow they thought would be returned.
This Caesar saw, and swift within his grasp
Uprose a ponderous axe, which downward fell
Cleaving a mighty oak that towered to heaven,
While thus he spake: 'Henceforth let no man dread
To fell this forest: all the crime is mine.
This be your creed.' He spake, and all obeyed,
For Caesar's ire weighed down the wrath of Heaven.
Yet ceased they not to fear. [...]
At the sight the Gauls
Grieved; but the garrison within the walls
Rejoiced: for shall men thus insult the gods
And find no punishment?

I recall Philippe's knowing smile as he first directed my attention to this passage, whose translation into French prose brings it closer than does Ripley's mock-antiquarian verse to the forest we both knew.

'No, the gods are not mocked. Caesar's men were right to be afraid. The blow *was* returned. You remember? ... It was by a blade that he died. Twenty-three stab wounds, in fact. And only a few years after his foolhardy antics in our forest. It really is sacred, you know.'

His eyes twinkled mischievously. But we both knew he had a point.

'Maréchal Brune didn't fare much better, either!'

He was referring to the events of 1815, when Brune – one of the first revolutionaries, but who later served under Napoleon – was recalled by the Corsican during his short-lived attempt to regain power, as he returned from Elba. Brune had been put in charge of the Army of the Var and had committed further desecration up at the grotto. What had been rebuilt so far after the Revolutionary onslaught was again destroyed.

Within a matter of months, the Maréchal had been assassinated at Avignon and his body thrown into the Rhône.

❧

It was Philippe who had insisted that I try taking an alternative path to the cave.

'An essential part of any pilgrimage,' he had stressed, 'is the element of ... well, *walking*! Of course, that used to be taken for granted in times gone by. But with so many holy places nowadays you can get there by car or plane or train. Here at the Sainte-Baume, whatever transport you use to arrive at the plateau, you have no option but to walk for at least an hour to get to the cave itself. And then perhaps another hour, if you are keen, to climb to the Saint Pilon. That's the tiny chapel that you've probably spotted, high above the mouth of the cave, on the very summit.'

I had visited the cave more than once in recent years, but made a mental note not to forget this Saint Pilon.

'You see,' Philippe had continued, 'on a pilgrimage you need a time of quiet preparation and recollection. And this enforced walk through the forest gives you just that! You need to go alone, though, in the morning. You'll find that the hour-long "bath" in the freshness of the forest will transform you. You'll feel different when you arrive. It can even be a time, you might say, of purification.'

It is true that making the ascent this way leads to an experience entirely different from that of yesterday's procession, with its loudspeakers and megaphones. Though it is rewarding to chant refrains and listen to Scripture readings in the company of hundreds of like-minded companions, it is equally important – yet far more difficult in today's world – to have the opportunity to clear one's mind, to sharpen one's senses, to feel oneself more in touch with the Eternal. As if to symbolize this process of purification, your body stops sweating once a certain height has been reached.

The forest eventually peters out as you come face to face with a perpendicular wall which rises sheer for another fifty metres or so and to which clings – impossibly, like a decorative magnet on a fridge – a building whose colouring blends with that of the rock itself. It is a small monastery, as architecturally daring as Meteora in Greece. As the path comes to an end at the foot of this cliff, you notice a beam protruding on your right, with a winch and pulley for hoisting up provisions. From this point 150 steeply rising steps bring you, after a few twists and turns, to a paved open space in front of the mouth of the cave. Turning your back on this for a moment to lean on the stone balustrade, you have the impression of being on a balcony overlooking the whole of Provence.

At almost 950 metres, the cave is a *haut lieu* in both senses of the word: a focal point of pilgrimage as well as being literally a 'high place'. Some twenty-nine metres deep, it has an average width of twenty-four. At its highest point, the roof is six metres from the floor. In summer it is best to rest a while and enjoy the view before going inside, for the interior temperature – a constant tweleve degrees – will come as a shock. This explains the pile of thick pullovers that can usually be found on a table to your left, these being for the benefit of those who omitted to bring warm clothing. In winter, on the other hand, the interior – at least, initially – seems invitingly warm.

Some English-speakers have thought that the word *baume* refers to balm. Presumably influenced in their opinion by Mary's role as myrrh-bearer at Christ's tomb, and also by the theory that identifies her as the woman who anointed his feet with costly perfume. There is indeed a French word *baume* having this meaning. However, it is masculine in gender. On the other hand, the feminine *la baume* is found in many place-names, meaning precisely the sort of cavern we have been describing – though here, by extension, the word is also used to refer to the mountain range as a whole. It is derived from the Provençal *baumo* or *baoumo*.* To give just three examples, there is the Rocher de La Baume near Sisteron, La Baume-Chapelue near Briançon east of Grenoble, and the Cirque-des-Baumes in the Cévennes. Clearly, the Sainte Baume – or *Santo Baumo*,

*When using them to refer to the area in general, I shall hyphenate the words *Sainte-Baume*; otherwise they refer more specifically to the cave itself.

as they say in Provençal – is *sainte* because of its association with Mary Magdalen. There is even another, much smaller Sainte Baume – just outside Lirac, which is near Châteauneuf-du-Pape. But this name is no older than the seventeenth century, when a local man is said to have discovered, in a crack of the rock, an image of the Virgin.

The sort of vertical or steep cliff (usually with a level top) in which the *baume* associated with Mary Magdalen is set is known by another Provençal-derived word: *un baou* or *baü*. Here the gender *is* masculine. There is, for example, Le Baou de Saint-Cassien at the eastern end of the Sainte-Baume range. Perhaps the most well-known example of this word's use, however, is in the name of the famous village near Arles, Les Baux.

The earliest extant detailed description of the cave – by Fra Salimbene, a Franciscan historian – dates from 1248. His *Chronicle* (covering the years 1167 to 1287) is one of the most useful sources for life in thirteenth-century Italy and France. He is generally considered to be an intelligent writer with a reasonably sound historical sense. Here, in my own translation, is his account:

> The cave in which St Mary Magdalen did penance for thirty years is at a distance of fifteen miles from Marseilles. I myself slept there for one night, immediately after her feast day. It is in a very high rocky mountain and in my opinion is actually large enough (if I remember correctly) to hold a thousand people. In it are three altars and a supply of water that has trickled down similar to the pool of Siloam. The route up to it is very beautiful. Outside, next to the cave, is a church in which there lives a priest. The mountain above the cave looks as high as the baptistery of Parma. The cave itself is so high above the plain that in my opinion (if I remember correctly) three Asinelli towers from Bologna would not suffice to reach it. The result is that the large trees below look like nettles or clumps of sage. Because the region is completely uninhabited, the women and noble ladies who travel there from Marseilles for devotional purposes take with them asses laden with bread, wine, pies, cakes, fish and such other supplies as they wish.

Ita elevata est a planitie terrae ... 'so high above the plain'. The famous twelfth-century Asinelli tower measures 97.6 metres, so Salimbene must be understood as saying that the grotto is 300 metres or so above the surrounding plateau. Consulting a detailed map, we find that the Hôtellerie is at 670 metres, the mouth of the cave at 946. Salimbene's description is remarkably accurate.

Some have thought that his estimate of the number of people the cave can accommodate is excessive. Yet he is quite correct, as I can vouch from personal experience. Indeed, the website of the Ecological Museum – in advising visitors as to the number of people the grotto can accommodate – states 'about 1,000'. It should be pointed out that the cave has two parts, a lower and an upper. Furthermore, in his day there would have been no chairs or pews to get in the way. Such seating was only introduced in the late Middle Ages, even in regular churches. Up here they will have been a later innovation still.

As for the baptistery in Parma, where Salimbene was born, it is one of the most important medieval buildings in Italy. His estimate is again remarkably accurate, for this octagonal structure of pink marble, separate from the cathedral next to which it stands, is twenty-six metres in height (not including the spires). Such a large baptistery as this was useful in the early Middle Ages, when baptisms still took place only once or twice a year and when the candidates were numerous. Begun in 1196 and not completed until just over a hundred years later, the overall structure would nevertheless have been complete in 1248, the time of Salimbene's visit to the Sainte Baume. It would indeed have been a topical point of reference.

If we ignore the early nineteenth-century restoration of the interior, necessitated by the repeated Revolutionary acts of vandalism, and if we also ignore the modern embellishments, Salimbene's description of the site is still valid today. The attractive walk through the forest, the priest-guardian, the capacity and dimensions, the supply of fresh water, the implied reference to a pilgrim path from Marseilles together with the distance from that town, and the bringing of provisions. The route from Marseilles would be the one nowadays known as the *Chemin de Giniez*, the one that dates back to pre-Christian times when Greeks from Massalia would come on pilgrimage to this sacred area, and before them the Celto-Ligurians. It follows the course of the River Huveaune, passing through the village of Saint Zacharie.

As for the bringing up of provisions, I am reminded of yesterday's gargantuan spread that was offered to the hundreds of pilgrims. Once the lengthy procession and services were completed, this was laid out on trestle tables on the terrace in front of the entrance to the cave.

I playfully wondered whether we might be offered any *madeleines*. (Not the small cakes made famous by Proust and which are named, not after the saint but apparently after the cook who invented them. Rather, *madeleines* in its less well-known meaning: those varieties of fruits – grapes, pears, plums, peaches – which ripen around the date of Mary's feast day.) As in Salimbene's day, the food and drink had been painstakingly brought up by women from Marseilles, plus one or two husbands. From Toulon and Saint-Maximin as well. Every last crumb of it. This is done several times a year, for the major feasts.

Salimbene's comparison with the Pool of Siloam is particularly interesting. The water that collects in the Sainte Baume cave he calls a *stilicidium*, a word often used to describe water collected from gutters and drainpipes. It comes from a verb meaning to drip or trickle. In fact, this is exactly how water gets here in this karstic limestone area. Although, in his reference to Siloam, he uses the word *fons* (a spring), it seems to me that he does so loosely and perhaps for the sake of lexical variety. For neither there nor here is there an actual spring or fountain. Of Siloam, the Latin New Testament uses the word *natatoria*, conveying the idea of a bathing place. There is, of course, no such pool in the cave; yet the way the water is collected and supplied is in both places identical. At Siloam it comes via an underground conduit from a spring on the other side of the eastern hill of Jerusalem. Here too the water – that is, the drinking water, not that which drips from the cave's ceiling – is captured and fed through a pipe. The four monks currently resident in the monastery often use it to supplement their meagre water rations. There is not enough, however, to provide for a public toilet.

It is in John's Gospel that Siloam is mentioned. As Jesus was walking along, he saw a man who had been born blind. He spat on the ground and made some mud with the spittle. Then he rubbed the mud on the man's eyes and said, 'Go and wash your face in the Pool of Siloam.' He went, washed his eyes, and had his sight restored. Legend has it that here, too, there is a connection with the Sainte Baume. For according to tradition, the man's name was Sidonius and it is after him that the so-called 'spring' in the cave is named. Indeed, the exceptionally pure quality of its water is said to make it ideal for eye infections and diseases. The connection does not stop there, however. For the Sidonius of the New Testament is also said to have been among the party that came to Provence along with Mary Magdalen. He is even said to have succeeded Maximin – another member of the party – as second Bishop of Aix.

❧

Looking up from the plateau at the monastery, you notice – high above it on the very crest and a little to the left – what looks like a doll's house, or even a hat box. At almost 1,000 metres, this is the Saint Pilon. To reach it requires up to another hour of walking. The going now gets rougher. Soon you are up to the last of the *oratoires*. These wayside shrines were erected in 1516. Originally there were seven, starting down at Nans, spaced out along the *Chemin des Rois*. Only four survive. Two metres tall, they depict sculpted scenes from Mary's life. Usually they are placed at sharp bends in the path where you can rest – you will want to do that! – and, as the word *oratoire* itself suggests, pray or contemplate for a while.

As you leave this last *oratoire* behind, the going gets decidedly tricky. The limestone rock is progressively more denuded of soil and vegetation until soon you are walking on slanting, slippery outcrops as polished as any marble surface. But when you finally catch a glimpse of what lies over the summit, it is like surfacing in a different climate after having risen from the depths of the ocean. The mountain slopes gradually away to the south, gleaming white, the few scrawny bushes that can cling to it smelling sweet. The path up from the cave has led you gradually to the left away from the sheer wall that rises above the mouth of the cave. To reach the Saint Pilon, you must now turn right and track west along the crest of the ridge until you are again over the monastery.

The term 'Saint Pilon' nowadays refers to a tiny chapel, usually locked and situated so near the edge of the cliff that to walk round behind it can cause vertigo in even the most sanguine of pilgrims. The present construction dates from 1618, but is not the first to have been built here. In 1474 Hans von Waltheym included in the account of his pilgrimage a brief description of an earlier chapel. The belief was, he added, that anyone who circled the building nine times would thereby obtain an indulgence. He himself could only manage once round, so dizzy did he become. By the time Jerome Münzer came, in 1495, the required number had dropped to three. This he managed easily. However, anyone who tries the same thing today should bear in mind that in those days the small protective parapet had not yet been built. Even so, stepping close to the edge can be an awesome experience. Especially when – even at the height of a hot summer – the wind whistles as it catches the edge of the cliff, like an invisible giant blowing on a blade of grass held between his thumbs. Several people, in fact, have fallen to their deaths along this crest.

Not far from the chapel, on the rocky terrain can be seen what looks like the imprint of horseshoes. The story goes that in the fourteenth century two Florentine merchants were making their way north from Toulon. By the time night fell, they had lost their way, but tried to cross the Sainte-Baume. At a certain point the horses stopped dead and refused to go any further, leaving the merchants no choice but to camp there for the night. As the sun rose next morning, they saw to their horror that they were on the very edge of the precipice, saved by their mounts. The horses would clearly not have left an imprint by themselves. Perhaps the merchants carved them on the rock in recognition and thanksgiving. They are certainly said to have donated two statues of horses to the chapel by way of ex-votos. Perhaps there is another explanation, for I had seen such 'horseshoes' on one of the *oratoires* on the way up; and was to see them again on walls and pillars in the basilica and its crypt in Saint-Maximin. Of which, more later.

Just to the east of the chapel, and much older than it, was the original *pilon.* This stele is said to have marked the precise spot to which Mary, according to legend, was transported daily by angels. From Waltheym's account, we learn that it was still standing in the late fifteenth century. I knew from Philippe that it had never been an erected column or pillar, as is often thought. There is such a thing – confusingly known as the Petit Saint Pilon – by the side of the main road down into Saint-Maximin, at the intersection of the old Via Aurelia. It is no older than the seventeenth century and commemorates what is said to have been the last meeting of Mary with Bishop Maximin, as she came down from her cave in the knowledge that her death was imminent. The one on top of the Sainte-Baume, however, will have been a *pieloun*, as Philippe put it, using the Provençal phrase: *Sant Pieloun*. In other words, a pillar-shaped rock naturally sculpted by the elements. Like a large boundary stone.

'Like the *Pilon du Roi* in the Chaîne de l'Étoile,' he had said. 'North of Marseilles.'

I remembered that this had been the title and subject of one of Cézanne's paintings. Such types of strangely shaped *pieloun* can also still be seen to the north-east, on the

Montagne de la Loube. One impressive example from there features on the cover of the IGN detailed map of the Sainte-Baume area. Certainly the conditions here are right; for the rocky surface on this side of the mountain is known as *lapiaz* by geologists. That is, outcrops of small pillars, cones or blocks of carbonate rock. Nowadays it is a question mostly of blocks, with which care must be taken, if one is not to sprain one's ankle. No sign of the original *pieloun* now remains. Weather and winter lightning eventually put paid to it at some time in the past.

Perhaps there was a link here with the pre-Christian worship that is associated with standing stones. Perhaps that is why a chapel was built up here, next to it, in the first place. To Christianize it. No one knows the date at which this might have been done. Certainly at least shortly after 1295, the date the Dominicans were installed in Saint-Maximin. Yet other monks had been in the area, guarding the memory and relics of Mary Magdalen since at least the fifth century, as we shall see.

❦

Whatever one's reasons for making such a climb as this – sacred or secular – certain feelings will be common to anyone who admires the views from the summit. Literally and perhaps spiritually, one can see further; the same things are viewed from a different perspective; you appreciate how all the details fit together.

'It is up at the Saint Pilon that any pilgrimage should culminate,' Philippe had remarked. 'It's the last of what I always see as the three parts. First, you have the purifying walk through the sacred forest. Then the visit to the cave which is a sort of tomb, if you like, reminding us of Christ's tomb. And last of all you have the Saint Pilon. It's been compared to Mount Thabor. You remember, the place where three of the disciples saw Christ transfigured.' It was an appropriate comparison. I recalled the moment when I first popped my head over the crest of the ridge, and of how the sudden whiteness of the rock and the light had taken my breath away.

As you look north over the forest, directly opposite is the Mont Aurélien, so called because the Via Aurelia passed by its foot. Beyond lies the Sainte-Victoire. On certain very clear days in winter, one can make out the snowy summits of the Ventoux. A little to the right is the Lubéron. Further to the right still and in the distance are the Mercantour and then Oisans in the Alps. On the horizon to your left are the Alpilles. Closer to, is the Garlaban rising above Aubagne. Turning to the south, you have the Massifs of the Estérel and Les Maures, Mont Faron just outside Toulon, the Bec de Cassis, and the whole of the Var coastline. On some days even Corsica.

Perhaps it was the air or the exhilaration, but as I looked out on my first ascent, fascinated by the sight of the Mediterranean shimmering like silver in the distance, a mere eighteen kilometres away at La Ciotat, I couldn't help wondering whether Mary Magdalen really had sailed its waters to land on these shores. Whether she did or not, was it at least feasible?

2

Massalia/Massilia First-Century Marseilles

Marseilles – still a busy port and the second most important city in France after Paris, than which it is much larger – is today rejuvenated and refreshed. After decades of depopulation, people are returning in their thousands.

As for the first century, if Mary Magdalen did come here, she would have been setting foot in a city that already boasted a prosperous and cultivated past, a city – the oldest in France – that was already 600 years old. As we have seen, Massalia was founded around 600 BC by merchant settlers from the Ionian city of Phocaea in Asia Minor, as a trading post in the western Mediterranean. Its situation was excellent. Near the mouth of the Rhône – with its access to northern Europe – it was at the same time far enough away from the delta to be relatively free of the diseases which such swampy places harboured. The colony developed rapidly, especially after 540 BC when the home city of Phocaea was destroyed by the Persians.

From the successful centre that Massalia became, Greek culture – including the introduction of olive trees and vines – spread to its satellites along the coast. From Ampurias to the west, in what is now Spain, to La Ciotat, Hyères, St Tropez, Antibes, Nice and Monaco to the east. As well as trading with the Orient and Egypt, the city's merchants despatched goods up the Rhône to the Atlantic. Based on such commerce, its simple yet stable institutions were cited as good examples by Aristotle, Cicero and Strabo.

Tensions with the Celto-Ligurian tribes of the interior caused the Massalians to seek an ally. Around 125 BC they fixed on up-and-coming Rome. At their request, the Romans defeated these local tribes and consul Sextius Calvinus founded the town of Aquae Sextiae, the future Aix-en-Provence. Roman roads and domination spread inexorably across the new *Provincia*. Particularly so after 102 BC, when consul Gaius Marius secured a celebrated and decisive victory over yet more threatening tribes – Teutonic now – just outside Massalia. It is a victory that resonates down to modern times, one that explains the local popularity of the forename Marius. In 58 BC the province began to be administered by a young consul called Julius Caesar.

Throughout this Romanization, Massalia retained a comfortable self-governing status until 49 BC, the year its leaders made the mistake of siding with Pompey against Caesar in the Roman Civil War.

Caesar removed from the defeated city its control of all the territory which had previously belonged to it. The new military colony and naval base of Fréjus (*Forum Julii*) received all the lands to the east, while the west as far as the Rhône went to Arles, the commercial port and centre of naval construction developed in 46 BC by Caesar for his veterans. The political power of Massalia – which now became known by the Latin version of its name, Massilia – became minimal. The city continued to flourish, however, and to retain its superiority as a centre of learning where Greek language and culture were passed on. Its university was renowned even in Rome. Agricola (born *c.* 40 AD) – who went on to become Governor of Britain – was educated here, when his father was stationed at Fréjus. In his *Life of Agricola*, Tacitus describes how his father-in-law was 'guarded from the enticements of the profligate' by having been brought up in a 'place where refinement and provincial frugality were blended and happily combined'.

As Caesar had intended, Arles – which had offered him ships during his siege of Massilia – displaced it as the main port.

Roman Arles was built on a rocky promontory and surrounded by water – that of the Rhône but also, to the east and south-east, that of the many lakes and swamps similar to those found today in the nearby Camargue. Indeed the Latin name Arelate means 'near the marshes'. It had become easily accessible from the sea thanks to Marius (Caesar's uncle) who, in 104 BC, had dug a canal uniting the town with the Gulf of Fos, slightly to the west of Massilia. The father of Seneca's wife was a local ship owner. All in all, commercial expansion was assured and cosmopolitan Arles became one of the main depots and granaries of Rome. Some twenty languages, it is said, could be heard there. In short, Arles – and, despite its setbacks, Massilia too – was in regular maritime contact with the rest of the Empire. With Caesarea and Joppa, for example, in Palestine. References to its many corporations of sailors have been found – in documents or on monuments – in many places, including Beirut and Tyre.

First-century Massilia, then, was not in some strange or remote country. It was part of a privileged *Provincia Romana*, *the* province par excellence. Moreover, as seen, the historical and geographical context in no way argues against a journey there from Palestine. On the contrary, many such journeys were made by first-century travellers at a time, in the middle of the Pax Romana, when maritime traffic in the Mediterranean was probably even more busy than in our own day. The many finds being discovered by maritime archaeologists off the coast of Marseilles seem to confirm as much.

It is, then, quite possible – even probable – that in New Testament times Christianized Jews will have visited the area of Marseilles, where there was already an established Jewish community. Perhaps the much-travelled Paul himself came here. Certainly he intended to visit Spain, after making at least one break in his journey – in Rome, as he specifies in his Letter to the Romans (15:24). Maritime journeys were in any case typically made by plying along the coast, making regular stops at such ports as Marseilles. Along with Clement of Rome, writing some thirty years after Paul's death, many early Church Fathers believe that he did make the journey to Spain. Whatever the precise details, we must conclude that there would have been nothing impossible or unusual in other early followers of Christ making such a journey including (in AD 45/7, according to tradition) Mary Magdalen.

Psychologically, the motivation to travel was clear. Negatively, there was the official persecution suffered by followers of Jesus after the stoning of Stephen in *c.* 35 AD (Acts 7–8). Moreover, if Mary was indeed the sister of Lazarus, it becomes significant that, since many Jews were being converted 'because of him' and his miraculous salvation from the tomb, the chief priests were plotting to kill him as well as Jesus (John 12:10). Mary's enforced placing on a boat by the Jerusalem authorities (along with Lazarus, Martha and others) – as the legend has it – could simply be a colourfully symbolic expression of fact.

As for the detail that the boat had neither rudder nor sail – a common enough motif and one, interestingly, that figures in earlier Jewish tales that tell of how their communities came to be established in southern France – what neater way of conveying the idea that they had entrusted themselves to the workings of the Holy Spirit? Of course, the ship motif later became a symbol of the Church in a wider sense, as the etymology of the word *nave* reminds us.

Positively, there was the compelling final injunction of Jesus to be his witnesses 'unto the uttermost part of the earth' (Acts 1:8). (It is worth reminding ourselves that the Church in Alexandria claims Mark as its founder, while the Indian Christians of Kerala point to Thomas as their evangelizer.) Like so many other travellers at the time – when overland routes were less popular – Mary and companions might well simply have boarded one of the ships that regularly made the voyage.

It would seem likely that first-century Provence did have Christians among its population, even if only grouped loosely like those at nearby Rome to whom Paul wrote *c.* 58 AD and whose community he clearly indicates as having been in existence for some time already.

But is there any real evidence to support this? Given the lack of documents and monuments, some have maintained that the evangelization of Provence was slow and late, datable perhaps to the third or fourth century. It is true that official documents concerning Provençal churches only appear at the beginning of the fourth century: for example, the list of regional bishops – from Arles, Apt, Vaison, Orange, Nice, not forgetting Marseilles itself – who were present at the Council of Arles in 314.

It was only in 313 that Emperor Constantine, who had convoked the Council, had made Christianity definitively acceptable. One would not expect there to have been many official documents prior to that date, whether they survived or not. Furthermore, what survives is precisely that: what survives! Moreover, documentary evidence inevitably presupposes an earlier non-documentary stage.

The late Régine Pernoud, world renowned medievalist and *conservateur* for the Archives de France, pointed out that the Qumran manuscripts are a dazzling exception to the rule that hardly any documents survive from the beginning of our era. As she reminded us, in other contexts historians rely quite happily on later copies. Even for such a celebrated figure as Cicero (d.43 BC) the earliest manuscripts are no older than the eleventh or twelfth centuries! Nor should we forget that oral traditions are themselves evidence.

Nevertheless, documentary evidence does exist of forty-eight named Christians martyred under Marcus Aurelius at Lyons in AD 177. Interestingly, half of them seem to have originally come from the eastern Mediterranean. An impressive, detailed eyewitness account is preserved in the *Ecclesiastical History* of Eusebius (compiled *c.* 323 AD). It takes the form of a letter, accepted as genuine by all historians, written by the Christians of Lyons (and Vienne) to their co-religionists in Asia Minor and Phrygia. Among the martyrs were the aged Pothinus, the town's first bishop, and a young female slave called Blondine, whose fortitude was outstanding. Pothinus – like his successor, Irenaeus – came from Asia Minor. Both seem to have known Polycarp, Bishop of Smyrna and a living link with the Apostles. Pothinus is believed to have been trained by Polycarp and sent by him to Lyons in the middle of the first century. It seems reasonable to suppose that there were groups of Christians there prior to this. If such were the situation in Lyons, even earlier dates can be posited for Arles and Marseilles, from where the new religion presumably spread up river.

As for funeral monuments, one would not expect to find any from the first or second centuries pertaining to a religion that was struggling to gain official acceptance. Moreover, it was only at the start of the second century that sarcophagi began to be used, even by wealthy pagan families, as the practice of cremation gradually fell into disuse. And only in the third century that burial as opposed to incineration became the norm throughout the empire. The well-off sections of society, the sort of people able to order marble coffins that would survive to our day, were in general the last to be Christianized. Although most sarcophagi were sculpted in Rome, a regional workshop did exist at Marseilles.

As recently as 2004 in the Rue Malaval in the heart of Marseilles, during the construction of a car park, an early Christian necropolis of some 230 graves was discovered, grouped round a church measuring some forty by eighteen metres. In the apse were two important tombs, being lead coffins inside a marble structure. Archaeologists also discovered that an aperture had been specially created, designed to allow a liquid (presumably oil) to flow down onto the lead and thus to become sanctified by contact with the tombs of what were undoubtedly revered persons, probably martyrs. A lead pipe protruding from the base of the structure allowed the liquid to be collected again. Though the earliest sections date only from the fifth century, the discovery is a reminder that much remains yet to be unearthed in Provence. Fourth-century sepulchres are, of course, to be found on display at such places as Arles and Apt.

As for the third century, one of the most interesting yet little-known archaeological exhibits can be seen at *La Roquière*, the *Co-opérative Vinicole* of La Roquebroussane, a village at the foot of the Sainte-Baume range, to the east. Its red wine is excellent, and cheap. When I last visited, notices on the outside walls had been posted in an attempt to counter the ignorance and myths surrounding Provence's *rosé* varieties. That they give you a headache; that they are a mixture of red and white; that they are an inferior by-product of the red. Yet when you go inside, whatever you order, it is a visit to the ancient tomb that you should first ask to sample. Slipping behind the sales counter, you will be led to small chamber, cool even in the summer months, and there you will find the skeleton of what has been certified to be a female some 1.57 to 1.64 metres in height. Discovered a decade or so ago during extension work, the remains are dated to the second half of the third century or the beginning of the fourth. There is no evidence that this was a Christian burial. Nor was it a particularly expensive one, the body having been enclosed by *tegulae* (tiles) rather than a sculpted marble coffin.

Yet one such, and a Christian one, was long ago discovered at La Gayole less than ten kilometres away between Brignoles and Tourves, just off the RN 7, the old Via Aureliana. Dating from the early third century, it is the oldest Christian monument to have been found in France and, such is the quality of the work, of international renown. Though there is still an archaeological site at La Gayole, the sculpted part of the sarcophagus can now be seen in the museum at Brignoles.

In Marseilles can be seen an early Christian epitaph from roughly the same period. The inscription refers to a Volusianus, son of Eutyches, and a Fortunatus – both of whom, 'faithful to God', were burned as martyrs. An anchor – symbol of Christian hope – terminates the inscription. This plaque is on display in one of the crypts of the ancient Abbaye Saint-Victor, where it was first found. Nearby are several third-century tombs discovered here in 1965. The dating of these to the time of the severe persecution that occurred under Decius (249–251) was made easier by the finding, set in the mortar that sealed the tombs, of a coin bearing his effigy.

First-century Provence was culturally different from Gaul as a whole. It had long been a land of coming and going, of exchanges, of hospitality. Like Palestine itself, it was a crossroads of civilizations and peoples: Ligurians, Celts, Greeks, Romans, Egyptians and Semites. In short, it is by no means fanciful to claim that Provence began to be Christianized at this early date. Equally, as seen, it is feasible that Mary Magdalen could have travelled here. What, then, of the tradition that says that she did indeed come? What exactly does it claim? Disregarding for the moment later embellishments, the story in essence is as follows.

On account of persecution by the Jerusalem authorities against followers of Jesus, particularly against his close friends, Mary surnamed Magdalen came by boat to the Rhône delta. With her came her brother, Lazarus, her sister, Martha, Maximin, one of the 72 disciples mentioned in Luke's Gospel (10:1), and several other people. The group eventually dispersed: Martha to Tarascon; Mary and Lazarus to Marseilles where Mary preached in the square in front of the Temple to Diana (Artemis) and where Lazarus eventually became bishop. Mary then moved with Maximin to Aix, where they continued their evangelizing mission, Maximin becoming first Bishop of Aix. Eventually, Mary retired to a cave in the mountain range now known as La Sainte-Baume and ended her days there as an anchorite.

Can any of this be true?

In attempting to answer this question, I shall – for reasons of cohesion and clarity – concentrate on Mary herself. Her supposed companions deserve an investigation of their own.

3

A Question of Identity

So much good there is
Deliver'd of her, that some Fathers be
Loth to believe one woman could do this;
But think these Magdalens were two or three.
(John Donne, *To the Lady Magdalen Herbert*)

It is not difficult to remember the first time I met Frère Philippe. I had arrived at the Maison Marie Magdelaine one hot afternoon in late July as arranged and had been shown into the reception room. Displayed on every available inch of flat space were publications, newsletters and other such documents. I made a note to check whether among them there might be any items relevant to my investigation that I had not yet consulted.

The chance to do so came sooner than expected; for, when Philippe himself appeared – in mufti – it was to ask whether I would mind waiting a while. After the briefest of introductory remarks – he is not a man to stand on ceremony – he took the *Gauloise* cigarette from his lips and asked whether I fancied a beer.

'Une bière, ça vous dit quelque chose?'

He wouldn't be long, he explained. I could, he pointed out, look at the various interesting publications that lay about.

'You see, it's the Tour de France. They're just about to arrive at the finishing line. I'm sure you wouldn't want me to miss that!' he added with a glint in his eye.

A true Frenchman, I thought. And one with his feet on the ground. No po-faced aesthete, him! Nor someone likely to look kindly on fairy tales. A good sign, surely.

Some thirty minutes later, after we had settled into conversation, I was confirmed in my belief that this engaging if unconventional Dominican was exactly the person I needed to meet. A distant relative of St Margaret Mary Alacoque, he struck me as being a naturally religious soul yet, more importantly, one completely devoid of religiosity.

When we met, Philippe had been at the Sainte-Baume for twenty years, fifteen of them as *gardien* at the cave.

'I remember,' he said with a smile, 'how one of my Dominican brothers had tried to advise me when I first took up my post. "Philippe," he said, "be careful not to make yourself look ridiculous. Marie-Madeleine? There's not much actually known about her. And nowadays most scholars think the traditional view of her is a mixing up of three separate women. As for her coming to Provence, official historians have established that it's merely a pious legend going back no further than the eleventh century. Be careful!"'

'And were you?' I asked.

He smiled again, infectiously.

'I was! Careful to study the matter … carefully! For twenty years I have been searching out and collecting every possible document on Mary Magdalen herself and on the Sainte-Baume. So many pieces of a giant puzzle! I've done a lot of thinking, too. And writing! More than fifteen *Cahiers* so far. A pious legend? Well, even those who believe that's all there is to it still need to pinpoint its origins – dates, places, authors. How did it suddenly arise one day? Actually, the critics – though they pride themselves on being "scientific" – are not very convincing on this.'

He tossed the packet of *Gauloises* onto the table, tapped it, then looked up again.

'You know, I took up this habit when I was drafted into the army. During the fighting in Algeria …'

Before examining the historicity of the legend itself, then, I realized that I must first face the problem of identity. What do we really know from the *bona fide* Gospels about Mary Magdalen? Given the difficulty of reconciling certain passages, it is a question that has taxed the minds of commentators since the end of the second century. Briefly put, the problem is one of deciding whether or not the Mary Magdalen of Provençal tradition (and of popular tradition in general) is an amalgam of more than one woman, a fictional character.

The Provençal account takes it for granted that she is none other than Mary the sister of Martha and Lazarus. Assumed, too, is her identity with the unnamed female 'sinner' of Luke who, like Martha's sister, anoints Christ. How many Marys were there? One, two, or three? After all, if the Provençal tradition encapsulates a case of mistaken identity, it is hardly worth investigating at all.

In recent years, as Philippe had said, the view that the relevant Gospel passages do indeed refer to three different women has become popular – more, it seems to me, for cultural reasons than any other. Yet, if there is one thing that is certainly beyond question it is that the texts themselves will never afford definitive proof either way.

I was to meet another Dominican against a Tour de France background a few days later, up at the cave in the small monastery *parloir* that affords a pilot's eye view of Provence. Henri-Dominique de Spéville could not be a more different character. Some twenty years younger than the retired Philippe and head of the band of four monks who now serve as *gardiens*, this former novice master exudes a balanced blend of rigour and warmth. Yet, despite their differences of character, it transpired that Frère Henri-Dominique agreed with Philippe on the main points.

As we pulled up our chairs at the solid mid-nineteenth-century table, I admired the wooden floor and savoured that feeling of well-being I always get, when surrounded by a roomful of furniture made entirely of natural materials.

Of the paintings and engravings on the walls, one in particular caught my eye. This was of a strangely dressed bearded figure standing against a stylized architectural background and surrounded by what seemed to be masonic symbols.

'Ah!' interrupted Henri-Dominique. 'The same mistake is made by many people. No, they are not masonic but simply tools. Look! These are pairs of dividers, and there's a mallet and a trowel.'

'But who is this strange person?' I asked.

'That's Maître Jacques. Legendary founder of the *Compagnons du Tour de France des Devoirs Unis.*'

Tour de France? Henri-Dominique had clearly seen the puzzled look that had come over my face.

'Don't worry,' he said. 'Many French people have never heard of them, let alone foreigners. Yet theirs is an ancient and worthy organization. In a way, I suppose it has something in common with the medieval guilds of craftsmen. That's the reason for the tools in the illustration.'

'Any kind of craft?' I asked.

'Just about,' replied Henri-Dominique. 'Skilled manual crafts, anyway. Let's see. Those connected with building, of course. Masons, stone carvers, carpenters, plasterers. But also coachbuilders, gunsmiths, glassworkers, engravers and woodcutters. In the past blacksmiths and farriers. Mmm ... Well, chefs de cuisine, of course. Then there's clockmakers, goldsmiths, cabinetmakers, printers, potters ... basket-makers, weavers ... photographers, too.'

'Really!' I said.

'One of their aims is to keep alive the ancient skills and to pass on the traditional methods.'

'So it isn't just a kind of all-embracing trade union?' I asked.

'Not at all!' he replied. 'Not if you're referring to such things as conditions of work or pay. No, there's the pride in one's craft, first. For its own sake. Then you have the other two pillars on which the *Compagnonnage* is founded. *La*

Fraternité. Apprentices are encouraged to experience something of communal life. In fact, there are special establishments – *maisons*, each with its "Mother" – where they can find food and lodging. Personal morality is stressed as well. When they have finished their training and successfully completed their "masterpiece", then comes *le Voyage*.'

Travelling? Before I had decided to raise the topic, Henri-Dominique continued.

'I suppose you're wondering about this *Tour de France*,' he asked.

'Well, yes,' I answered. 'I don't quite see how it fits with what you have already told me. Obviously, nothing to do with cycle races,' I added.

'Well, no. Again, this tradition too must owe something to the Middle Ages, the time when the great cathedrals were being built, when craftsmen would travel from town to town searching for greater technical knowledge and skill.'

He stood up.

'Wait, I'll show you an interesting book recently written by one of their members. Just a second! Have a look through these binoculars while you're waiting.'

He handed me a large, high-specification pair that had been lying on the windowsill.

'See if you can find the cemetery!'

As he left the room, I attempted to do just that. Eventually, I managed to locate the Hôtellerie, which seemed seven leagues away and no more imposing than a toddler's Lego construction. The tiny cemetery which I knew to be beside it took longer to bring into focus. Individual tombstones escaped me; but I did make out the telltale presence of the cedars of Lebanon.

'Did you find it?' Henri-Dominique was back with a swirl of his white robe. 'That's where we *gardiens* are buried,' he smiled.

The book was attractive enough and well illustrated. I noted that it dealt in large measure – as its title announced – with the links between the *Compagnons* and the Sainte-Baume. In fact, it contained some of the most stunning photos of the area that I'd seen. My next question asked itself.

'Is there a link, then, between them and this place?'

'Of course! Mary Magdalen is their patron too, just as she is for us Dominicans. It connects with what I was saying about the moral aspect of their organization. Not just as concerns their own personal behaviour, but their approach to their work and to life in general. Moral, yes ... even spiritual. You see, once qualified, each *Compagnon* makes his *Tour de France* and one of the most important journeys – the final stop, in fact – is right here. Every newly qualified *Compagnon* is expected to make the pilgrimage at least once in his life. And it's my job to receive them. So I've come to learn more about what motivates them.'

I realized it was high time I got out my notebook.

'They come,' he continued, 'to ask the help and protection of Mary Magdalen. You remember the visit of Christ to the house of Mary and Martha in Bethany?'

I noticed that Henri-Dominique – or, at least, the *Compagnons* whose point of view he was relaying – instinctively identified these two Marys.

'Well, to be a *Compagnon* you must not simply love your craft, you must learn to have a respect for the material that you work with and fashion. I would myself see it as part of a respect for God's material creation in general. Yet that is just the first stage.'

Never tiring of appreciating the highly developed aesthetic sense of the French – reflected at a humble level in any chemist's or any cake shop – I was eager to hear what he would add.

'Yes, that's a matter of giving meaning to one's craft, one's trade. But to stop there would be restricting oneself to the merely visible, the practical, the level of the bustling hostess Martha. It was Mary, you remember, who chose what Christ described as "the better part". It is this contemplative aspect of Mary that the *Compagnons* seek to bring to their work. They try to rise above the senses. Not to deny them, but to purify them. And there is no doubt that a pilgrimage up to this cave can help in this.'

I nodded, recalling my own feelings each time I made the slow climb through this unsullied landscape.

'They aim to give meaning not just to their workmanship but to their life. They transform visible materials, but there should also be an inner invisible tranformation of oneself.'

We both fell into silence for a moment.

'You said it was your job to receive them. Could you tell more about that?'

'Oh, I was thinking in particular of what they call their colours and the special register we keep, for them to sign once they have got here. And the special stamp we use to formalize the inscriptions.'

Henri-Dominique took up the book again and turned to several illustrations of the *couleurs* he had referred to. These took the form of broad sashes of silk or velvet, decorated with floral motifs and having golden fringes. He pointed to a relevant passage in the text, where it was explained how, on the eve of his adoption, each young candidate receives one of these. It will contain a symbol specific to his own craft but also another design, whose significance might as yet elude him. It shows two figures: one a woman kneeling, with arms outstretched towards a man who is holding a spade in his left hand. Behind them is the mouth of a cave. Underneath the scene, the words *Noli me tangere* ('Do not cling to me!') make clear that it is a representation of the meeting between Mary Magdalen and the risen Christ, whom she has mistaken for the gardener.

'Last Februrary,' Henri-Dominique continued, 'a special delegation came with their President and the local Mayor. That was after the reopening of the cave. I think you know it had been closed for several years after having become unsafe. Well, they came to entrust us again with the special stamp and register for those of their members who make the pilgrimage. Of course, as Superior, I had to welcome them officially and make a speech of acceptance.'

Things were becoming clearer. I could think of no British equivalent to such an organization.

'Have you seen the stained-glass windows by the entrance to the cave?' enquired Henri-Dominique. 'They were made by a *Compagnon*. He's been renewing the scenes carved in stone in the wayside *oratoires*, too.'

Time was passing and we both realized that we were in danger of losing sight of the main purpose of our meeting. I closed the book that lay before us, reminding myself to buy a copy, and searched in my shoulder bag for the letter I had promised to show Henri-Dominique.

It was from an old friend, then still alive and a senior monk at Simonas Petras monastery on Mount Athos. He had long ago sent me a small hollow cross to be worn under clothing around the neck, as is the Greek custom. Inside, he had placed a wad of cotton wool which had been in contact with his monastery's relic of Mary Magdalen: her left hand. I had written to him, telling him of my intention to investigate the Provençal tradition. In his reply he had focused on the question of her identity, expressing the standard Greek view that she could not be identified with Mary the sister of Lazarus nor with the sinful woman who appears in Luke's Gospel.

I was pleased to learn from Henri-Dominique that he himself was preparing a talk on this very question of identity. Pleased too to find we were in agreement that, despite what is often said and despite the official position of the Orthodox Church today, there never was in earlier centuries a clear-cut division of the sort that would posit a unanimous conflation of the three women among the early Latin Fathers as opposed to a unanimous separation of them among the Greek. Several of the most revered of the early Greek Fathers all suggest, for example, that Lazarus's sister Mary is the same woman as Luke's unnamed sinner.

We agreed too that, despite a post-Vatican II trend in some parts of the world to separate the women, this remains an area of freedom and legitimate debate, not a question of dogma.

When he had read the relevant part of my Athos letter, Henri-Dominique disappeared again, briefly.

He returned this time with a copy of an article by another Dominican – André Feuillet, a New Testament specialist.

'Here's an article from the *Revue Thomiste* on the very topic that interests you,' he said. 'I found it very useful in preparing my talk. You might find it helpful, too.'

Our conversation necessarily became somewhat detailed, but by the end of this particular stay at the Sainte-Baume I had become convinced of one thing. Whether or not Mary Magdalen ever came to Provence, she can justifiably be described as 'la femme coupée en morceaux', the woman hacked to bits. The phrase – a colourful riposte to those critics who insisted that the Magdalen of tradition was a composite of three separate people – was coined by Bruckberger, another Dominican, whose important 1950's book on the subject has never received adequate recognition. Its lengthy exegetical Appendices, in particular, are of considerable interest. (In my own Appendix, I give the main arguments advanced by Feuillet and Bruckberger, along with some considerations of my own.)

❧

It turned out that Philippe's first three *Cahiers* had themselves been devoted to precisely this question. I hadn't read them when I put my question to him.

'Supposing Mary Magdalen was indeed Luke's unnamed sinner, do you think she had been – as we so often hear – a prostitute?'

He nearly choked on his *Gauloise*. 'Now you've really got me going!' he exploded. 'Nowhere does it say she was a prostitute. Yet people have turned her into a *vieille pute*, an old bag!'

'I agree,' I interrupted. 'But you must nevertheless have an opinion on what Luke meant by describing the woman as "a sinner in the city".'

'Of course, as I was about to say ... Well, I suspect she was *de bonne famille*, intelligent but *mal vue*. Unconventional – like Jesus! A free spirit. Couldn't tolerate the shallow rituals and hypocrisy of people like her critics. She didn't "keep the rules" ... So, she was "a sinner". There are many people like her today. I've often encountered them. They may have been baptized as children, but they stay away from church. Why? Because they are sickened by the hypocrisy and lack of love they have met with in certain church-goers.'

He paused to stub out his cigarette.

'You know, I imagine the occasion when she bursts in as being a *dîner très chic.* Think of the self-righteous remarks that would be made as they bundled her out of the room! You can see Jesus putting up with so much ... But by the time they came to the *fromage*, I can well imagine that he might have pushed back his chair, stood up, slapped down his napkin and walked out with a"Bonsoir, Messieurs les censeurs!"'

I couldn't help laughing at this vivid yet apt recreation of the scene.

But Philippe was leaning forward with a conspiratorial look.

'Who knows?' he added. 'Perhaps Mary was waiting for him outside. She certainly became a devoted follower from then on. I wonder what they might have said to each other ...'

He suddenly stopped, as if trying to eavesdrop across the centuries.

After a minute or so, he shook out another cigarette. I took the opportunity to continue my questioning.

'I can see from what you have already said that you believe that we are talking about one woman, not three.'

'Well,' he said, shrugging his shoulders and opening wide his hands, 'I don't mind saying that I agree with St Augustine!'

He looked me straight in the eye before continuing, as if waiting for my reaction. My smile threw the ball back in his court.

'Look,' he went on, 'the two anointings – the one described by Luke at the beginning of Jesus' ministry and the one at the end in Bethany – *eh bien*, it seems quite reasonable, quite *vraisemblable* to believe that they were both performed by the same woman. Mary Magdalen, the sister of Lazarus, the sinner whose name Luke withheld.'

'And St Augustine?' I asked mischievously, for by the time of this particular conversation I had read Feuillet's article and knew what Augustine had written.

'You know, I can't see that he was wrong in suggesting that, at Bethany, Mary wished to perform again the events linked to that moment in the past when she was decisively converted. Perhaps, too, she did have a vague premonition of Jesus' approaching death.'

'He had been predicting it often enough,' I interrupted.

'Exactly! And she, more than the others, seems to me to have been the one who intuitively sensed what was unfolding. Anyway, whatever the precise facts, you don't need to be a psychologist to detect in these two extraordinary incidents the actions of what our Lacordaire described as "une seule âme"!'

He bent forward to extract an insect that had landed in his coffee. We were sitting in his garden at the time. Suddenly his eyes lit up again.

'This second anointing ... Do you think it was simply linked to Jesus' burial?'

'Well,' I replied, 'that's what he himself linked it to.'

'Of course! I'm not denying that. That is what he said. Yet people often forget that what Jesus *did* is just as important as what he said.'

'I agree wholeheartedly with that!' I volunteered. 'So many of his actions, in fact, are acted parables or fulfilments of prophecy.'

'Precisely,' Philippe replied. 'And we get one of those just after this anointing at Bethany ... In the very next verses of John's Gospel, in fact! Jesus enters Jerusalem ... in a way that testifies not just to his Messiahship but to his Royalty. What had Zechariah prophesied? "Lo, your king comes to you; triumphant and victorious is he, humble and riding on an ass, on a colt the foal of an ass, sitting on an ass's colt."'

He paused, waiting to see if I had got his point. We were

both in agreement that, even though such quotations had obviously been added *after* the events in question, Jesus himself had had them in mind beforehand. Yet I suspected that Philippe had something else up his sleeve.

'Royalty ...,' he continued. 'Remember that. Everyone knows that "Messiah" in Hebrew means "Anointed One". Now, although Jesus' *words* did link the Bethany anointing to his burial, his very next recorded *action* – at least, according to John – is his royal entry into Jerusalem. The way I see it, it was at Bethany that this symbolic royal act actually began!'

He finished his coffee.

'Not with the feet,' he quickly added, wiping his mouth. 'That's not how you anoint a king! No, the head! Which is exactly what Matthew and Mark say also happened at Bethany.'

I had to admit that he had a point. It was one that had never previously occurred to me in quite this way. Moreover, I later had occasion to recall his comments in quite a different context, back in England.

I had been mulling over the position of the Orthodox Church with regard to the question of identity. As I had mentioned to Henri-Dominique, it is often claimed that she insists on a strict separation of the three women. Yet her service books, at least, suggest that Mary of Bethany – whether or not she was Mary Magdalen – was the same person as Luke's unnamed sinner. In the Mattins texts for Wednesday in Great (or Holy) Week, one of the main themes is the commemoration of none other than this woman, who is described as wiping and anointing Christ's feet that she has wetted with her tears. Perhaps the most loved of all the texts of the day – the one by Kassiani the Nun (ninth century) – clearly identifies her as the woman of Bethany: 'The woman who had fallen into many sins [...] fulfilled the part of a myrrh-bearer and [...] brought sweet-smelling oil of myrrh to Thee before Thy burial'. Even the day chosen for this commemoration – Wednesday in Holy Week – seems to be an implicit reference to the anointing at

Bethany, which itself took place shortly before Christ's passion. Moreover – and this is what reminded me of Philippe's argument – other texts of the day describe her as anointing Jesus' '*royal* head' with myrrh.

I made a note to send Philippe a copy of them.

❦

All in all, I couldn't escape the conclusion that, psychologically, everything seemed to point to the three women as being one person. As Philippe had put it, it was *vraisemblable*. The character traits are constant: she is instinctively generous, but must continually suffer criticism and misunderstanding – whether by Simon the Pharisee, by her sister Martha or by Judas. Yet on each occasion she is defended and championed by Jesus.

And then there is the recurring reference to feet.

'It was Mary who [...] wiped his feet with her hair', writes John (11:2), obviously implying that this was the distinguishing characteristic by which the early community knew her. In the passage devoted to the unnamed sinner, feet are mentioned seven times. Clearly, Luke – like Jesus – was impressed by the attention given to them. Unlike Martha, she sits at these feet, listening to Jesus' teaching, just as she later sat patiently by his tomb. When Jesus approaches the grave of her brother Lazarus, it is at his feet that she throws herself. Meeting the risen Jesus, she again embraces his feet. There are many ways of identifying a person other than by using their name. Mary is unquestionably, as Bruckberger put it, 'the woman at the feet of Jesus'.

Pieced together, the various Gospel texts present what can only be termed a convincing consistency. Early in the ministry of Jesus, a woman is healed and pardoned; she becomes a loyal disciple who understands his message perhaps more than most, travelling with him and giving him material support; she anoints him for burial; is with him at the Cross as at the tomb; she is the first to see him risen and the first to announce the good news; she is among the unnamed women present at Pentecost.

It is difficult not to agree with Lacordaire's conclusion. 'Any division of this fame,' he wrote, 'is fanciful!'

4

Hair and Other Accretions

One cannot for long consult the paintings, statues and indeed the reliquaries of the Mary Magdalen of Provençal tradition without becoming aware of certain recurring features. She is as often as not naked, sporting body-length hair and, when not grovelling amid a flood of tears, is borne aloft by angels – seven times a day, according to some sources. She lived for thirty years in the cave without feeling the cold and without needing normal food. In addition, she was transported – shortly before her death, whose timing she predicted – down to the oratory at the foot of the mountain, there to be given communion before expiring and being buried by Bishop Maximin, who had originally travelled with her from the Holy Land. Further variations and additions exist; they seem to have grown along with the hair.

The account given in the thirteenth-century so-called *Golden Legend* is typical of the most developed versions; it is certainly the most widely known and is often used as a stick with which to beat the entire Provençal tradition.

The Golden Legend is merely a nickname, and a potentially confusing one. To begin with, one should use the plural since it is a vast compilation of the Lives of hundreds of saints – *Legenda Sanctorum* being the original Latin title – together with explanations of the feasts relating to Christ or the Virgin Mary, arranged according to the liturgical calendar. Moreover, these are not legends in the modern sense of 'fable'; but lections, readings, or lessons. Nonetheless, on account of its great popularity as well as the high value set on its content and message, the compilation acquired the name 'golden' almost at once.

The author, Jacobus de Voragine, was a saintly Dominican: a professor of theology, a chronicler and later – against his wishes – Archbishop of Genoa. One of the most learned men of his day, he was also author of a *Chronicle of Genoa* and a *History of the Lombards*. Far from being a gullible dupe, he often expresses reserve as to the value of his sources, whilst maintaining a proper belief in God's miraculous powers. Before dismissing his compilation as so much medieval myth-making, then, we should take care lest we become guilty of what C. S. Lewis called 'chronological snobbery'.

In the Preface to his 1910 translation, Teodor de Wyzewa, a polymath French writer of Polish origin, was one of the first to rehabilitate Voragine. He points out that Voragine was well aware that others before him had written lives of the saints and commentaries on the cycle of feasts. But these had been intended for clerks and theologians. Voragine's aim was to bring the treasures of Christian spirituality out from the libraries behind monastery walls, out into the streets and marketplaces in a clear but attractive form. Hence he deliberately writes in a simple Latin, though he was later to be mocked on this score by misguided Renaissance humanists and reformers.

Wyzewa points out that, however varied the different entries, all are inspired by the person and teaching of Christ. Thus, we are presented with a religion of compassion and consolation. Perhaps it was this, he suggests, rather than the more fanciful aspects, that most annoyed later critics. Especially in the seventeenth century, with its Jansenism and Protestantism, when an excessively human conception of God's justice caused many to feel it unwise to stress his indulgent goodness, and when it became the rule to frighten people rather than reassure them. It is, of course, a tendency which was not unknown in the nineteenth and early twentieth centuries. *The Golden Legend*, if not factually correct in every detail, is at least a more authentic witness than this to the true message of Christ.

Petrarch's poem, as seen in our Prologue, picks up most of the additions to the story. Yet, before we too adopt an overly condescending stance and dismiss them as nothing but poetical embellishments, it is worth remembering that, in themselves, they contain nothing that is necessarily nonsensical.

For example, the numbers of years Mary spent in isolation, almost always given as thirty, is surely modelled on the length of the hidden life of Christ, before he began his public ministry. Similarly, though it also has something to do with a concern for maturity, it is still traditional in the Eastern Church not to ordain men to the priesthood until they have reached this symbolic age.

With regard to Mary's imperviousness to external conditions, let us listen to Petrarch again:

> 'Tis said thou didst endure thrice ten Decembers,
> Not weakened by the frost nor cowed by dread,
> Since hunger, cold, and the hard bed of stone
> Were sweetened by the love and hope deep-seated in thy breast.

As for cold, few places can be crueller than northern Russia in winter; yet it was there that in the fourteenth century St Sergius built a hermitage, in total isolation in the midst of a virgin forest. Here is how one modern Russian writer, Nicolas Zernov in his *St. Sergius – Builder of Russia*, describes his struggle:

> Although it required exceptional strength of character to face unarmed the possible attacks of the beasts of the forest and to endure the burden of loneliness and complete isolation, all this was nothing compared to the main trial which St. Sergius had to suffer, that of the gales and frosts of a Russian winter. [...] Those who have experienced storms both at sea and in the Russian plains know how similar is the effect which these uncontrollable forces produce upon the human mind. The snow blizzard descends upon man with the sound of the

> roaring sea, blinding him, paralysing his mind and body, and crushing his will to survive. But, above all, [Sergius] had to pass through the trial of cold, the greatest enemy to life, which dominates the regions chosen as the place of his seclusion. It is impossible to describe to those who have not experienced it the benumbing effects which intense cold has upon human beings. It freezes the very blood, it kills the very desire to struggle and to live.

Nor did Sergius use a fire; yet, like the Mary Magdalen of tradition, he seems to have won through. For, Zernov continues,

> his biographer [a contemporary and disciple] tells us that through his long life he was never ill, that he had to the end the strength of two men [...] and that, above all, he remained singularly insensitive to cold, being able to wear the same shabby old cassock both in summer and winter.

The life of a later Russian hermit – one who was buried, as he requested, with an icon of St Sergius placed on his heart – affords further insight into this phenomenon. On a Thursday in late November 1831, a certain Nicholas Motovilov (a wealthy though philanthropic landlord) had an unusual experience in the company of St Seraphim of Sarov. Motovilov's handwritten account still exists. In the opinion of experts, the style of the manuscript preserves Seraphim's manner and way of speaking, indicating that it was committed to paper very soon after the event itself.

Seraphim was a prime example of what is known as a *staretz*. Literally, the word means an 'old man'. However, it came to be used of someone recognized as being of exceptional personal holiness and highly experienced in the inner spiritual life.

Motovilov had asked Seraphim to sum up for him the true aim of the Christian life. It was winter, but Seraphim had taken him to a forest glade near his hermitage. They were sitting on a recently felled tree trunk.

'Prayer, fasting, works of mercy – all this is very good,'

replied Seraphim, 'but it represents only the means, not the end of the Christian life. The true end is the acquisition of the Holy Spirit.'

The conversation continued for a while, but eventually Motovilov said, 'Father, you keep on saying that the grace of the Holy Spirit is the goal of the Christian life, but how or where can I see such a grace? Good works are visible, but can the Holy Spirit be seen? How can I know whether or not he is in me?'

'The grace of the Holy Spirit,' continued Seraphim, after further discussion, 'given at baptism in the name of the Father, and of the Son, and of the Holy Spirit, [chrismation or confirmation is administered immediately after baptism in the Orthodox Church] continues to shine in our heart as divine light in spite of our falls and the darkness of our soul.[...] It is by this ineffable light that the action of the grace of the Holy Spirit manifests itself to all those to whom God vouchsafes to reveal it.'

Then, after praying inwardly, Seraphim gripped Motovilov by the shoulders, saying: 'My friend, both of us at this moment are in the Holy Spirit, you and I. Why won't you look at me?'

'I can't look at you, Father, because the light flashing from your eyes and face is brighter than the sun and I'm dazzled!'

[...]

'What do you feel?' asked Father Seraphim.

'An amazing well-being,' Motovilov replied. As throughout, Seraphim cited frequently the words of Scripture to anchor the experience in Truth.

'Do you feel anything else, my friend?'

'I'm amazingly warm.'

'Warm? What are you saying, my friend? We are in the depths of the forest, in mid-winter, the snow lies under our feet and is settling on our clothes. How can you be warm?'

'It's the warmth one feels in a hot bath.'

'Does it smell like that?'

'Oh no, nothing on earth can be compared to this! There's no scent in all the world like this one!'

'I know,' said Seraphim, smiling. 'It's the same with me. I'm only questioning you to find out what you're discovering. It is indeed true, friend of God, that no scent on earth can be compared with this fragrance, because it comes from the Holy Spirit. By the way, you've just told me that you've been feeling the warmth of a hot bath, but look: the snow settling on us isn't melting, neither on you nor on me. That shows that the warmth isn't in the air but is within us. This is what the Holy Spirit causes us to ask God for when we cry to him: "Kindle in us the fire of the Holy Spirit!" Warmed by it, hermits are not afraid of winter hardship, protected as they are by the mantle of grace which the Holy Spirit has woven for them. [...] Didn't the Lord say: "The kingdom of God is within you"? This kingdom is just the grace of the Holy Spirit, living in us, warming us, enlightening us, filling the air with his scent. [...] At this moment we are with those whom the Lord mentions as not tasting death before they see the kingdom of God come with power. [...] Treasure this memory of the revelation given you of the fathomless loving-kindness of God who has visited us today.'

Motovilov – a hard-headed businessman, not some anonymous medieval compiler of stereotyped hagiographies – concludes as follows:

> From the instant when Father Seraphim's face became filled with light, the vision did not fade; the Staretz remained in the same position that he was in at the beginning of the conversation and this ineffable light went on shining all the time he was talking. I am prepared to take an oath on the truth of my words.

Not surprisingly, Iulia de Beausobre's book about Seraphim is entitled *Flame in the Snow*.

❧

Turning to Petrarch again, what are we to make of the following lines?

> He nourished thee for thirty years beneath this cliff.
> Ne'er needing mortal food for so long a time, thou wast
> Content with naught but divine nourishment and wholesome
> dew.

Are we really expected to believe that people can survive for any length of time without normal nourishment? Whether we believe it or not, examples abound down the centuries. Indeed, in selecting them one is spoilt for choice.

At the end of the twelfth century, for instance, in Cudot in Burgundy there lived a young peasant girl, Alpais, who was cured of a serious illness after a vision of the Virgin Mary. Alpais regained some measure of health, but remained an invalid without the use of her limbs. From then on her sole food was the Eucharist each Sunday. Things came to the attention of Bishop Guillaume of Sens, who promptly set up an investigation. When this confirmed the facts, he had a small church built next to her house so as to allow her to participate in the services via a window. As her reputation of holiness grew, so did her powers of intercession, with the result that Cudot became a place of pilgrimage. St Alpais died in 1211 but her Life was written while she was still alive, by a Cistercian monk who knew her well.

In the fifteenth century there is the Swiss example of St Nicholas of Flue. Some say that, had it not been for him, Switzerland as we know it – with all that it has come to symbolize in terms of neutrality and peace – would probably not exist.

When aged about fifty, Nicholas became incapable – until his death some twenty years later in 1487 – of eating or drinking. Having withdrawn to a hermitage, he too acquired a reputation as a spiritual guide. In 1481, when the confederacy of Swiss *cantons* were on the point of turning on each other in civil war, it was only as a result of his advice (sought in desperation by the priest who had been his confessor) that peace prevailed.

More recent still is the case of Alexandra Maria da Costa.

Born in a small village in northern Portugal in 1904, she was a strong, healthy girl. When aged fourteen, she was working at home with another girl as a seamstress. Three drunks entered the house and tried to rape them. Alexandra managed to escape by jumping from a window. The men took flight and fled. However, as she had fallen some four metres, her spine was irreparably damaged. Permanent, irreversible paralysis set in. From 1925 until her death in 1955, she remained bedridden. For the last thirteen years of her life she took no food or water except daily communion. When news of this spread, her family were accused of deception. Nonplussed, they agreed to an observation period of thirty-three days in the nearest hospital. This was supervised by a relay team of doctors and nurses, some of whom were very antagonistic. The head doctor, in particular, was openly hostile. At the end of the period, he accused his own nurses of having been deceived and ordered a ten-day extension. However, the final official medical report could not but confirm without reservation that Alexandra had abstained from food and liquid from 10 June to 20 July without any ill effects. 'The laws of physiology and biochemistry,' read the report, 'cannot account for the survival of this woman.'

One final example, closer still in time, should suffice to suggest that, whether or not this detail has been added to the Provençal legend at some later date, it is not *per se* an absurdity.

Marthe Robin died in 1981 in the village where she had been born, Châteauneuf-de-Gallaure, Lyons. For more than fifty years she was bedridden and completely paralysed, apart from being able to move her head slightly. She could eat nothing at all, and could not even take a sip of water. If doctors tried to force some down her throat, it came back up through her nostrils. Neither did she sleep. During the last forty years of her life she was blind. Moreover, for over half a century her only food was the Eucharist, once a week. Drawn by her exceptional spiritual gifts, tens of thousands – including philosophers, one a member of the *Académie*

Française – visited her in the small room to which she was confined for most of her life. Many of them are still alive.

❦

Here unseen by human eye, surrounded by angelic hosts,
Seven times a day for the canonical hours
Wast thou from thy bodily prison
Transported, and to hear the choirs of heaven in antiphonal chant
Found worthy.

Petrarch again. Passing over his sub-Christian description of the body as a 'prison' – a conceptual trap into which many before and since have fallen – it is his reference to Mary's being 'transported' that points us in the direction of what seems to be another improbable addition to the tradition.

Although Petrarch merely says that Mary was 'surrounded' by angels, some versions of the story insist that it was by their agency that she was lifted up – up to the summit of the Sainte-Baume, to the Saint Pilon where now stands the tiny chapel. The main reliquary in the Basilica of Saint-Maximin has four angels holding her aloft. Of course, the Mary Magdalen of the Gospels had already seen two angels at Christ's tomb. Yet how have such celestial beings entered the Provençal story? What, if anything, are we to make of them?

The reference to 'seven times a day' is easily accounted for, this corresponding to the monastic hours of Mattins with Lauds, Prime, Terce, Sext, None, Vespers, and Compline. When I asked Philippe for his views on this aspect of the tradition, he slapped his hand on the table and was off!

'You know, one old friend – a *Compagnon*, who comes here often – you've heard about the *Compagnons*, haven't you? . . . Well, he said to me one day. "Philippe, it's all very well researching and preserving the tradition, but don't you think this business of Mary's being carried up to the Saint

Pilon and then down to the town for her imminent death ... Well, don't you feel that this is one thing that could be dropped?" Do you know what my reply was?' Philippe added.

I couldn't wait to hear.

'I told him that this was the one thing above all that should *never* be dropped! He was quite surprised ...'

Philippe shook his head slowly and repeatedly. From the expression on his face, I gathered that he was frustrated at the inability of people to comprehend.

'What did Christ say to Mary in the garden? "I *ascend* to my Father and your Father." We are *all* called to ascend! But we won't get there by doing yoga or other such devices. People who promote that sort of thing are just swindlers! No, we're all sinners and none of us can "ascend" by relying on ourselves. We must *all* let ourselves be lifted up by angels!'

Inevitably, the burial hymn that follows the traditional Requiem service came to mind: *In paradisum deducant te Angeli.* May the Angels lead thee into Paradise.

'I see,' I ventured, 'that you agree with me that many people nowadays have lost a sense of the symbolic, in the deeper meaning of that word.'

'*Pouf*! Absolutely!' he replied. 'This transporting, for instance. If it were to be understood as a sort of celestial ski lift to take Marie-Madeleine up to the Saint Pilon literally ... well, it would have absolutely no meaning or value! We have landed on the moon but we are more stupid than our ancestors – or the medieval artists and pilgrims who came here. They weren't idiots! Or fundamentalists.'

'Don't you find,' I interrupted, 'that so-called fundamentalists usually turn out to be superficialists?'

I recounted a conversation I had had a few years previously with a couple of Jehovah's Witnesses who had knocked on my door. 'Do you believe,' they asked, 'that every page in the Bible is of equal worth?' I shook my head. 'Well,' they continued, 'do you at least believe that every word in the Bible is literally true?' 'It depends what you mean,' I had replied, without making myself understood. I still had one hand on my half-opened door and suddenly remembered the words of Jesus: 'I am the Door'. These I quoted aloud. 'I believe this to be true,' I explained, 'in the sense that Jesus is a point of access. But it is not true, if you think he is comparing himself to a few planks of wood with hinges attached.' Still getting nowhere, I brought the conversation to an end as politely as possible. Later that evening another verse from the gospels floated into my mind. From Luke 10, where Jesus is giving instruction to his disciples: 'Go not from house to house'. Should I, I wondered mischievously, have asked my visitors for their views on this?

Ski lifts. Philippe would never, of course, have denied that the history of Christian spirituality abounds with examples of levitation: St Cuthbert, St Bonaventure, St Francis Xavier, to name a few at random. Nor is it necessarily a supernatural phenomenon. Some say it is connected with biogravitational fields and a special kind of mental energy emitted by the brain. Whatever the case, with Christian saints there is no training programme, unlike with yogis, lamas or Brahmans. It happens unexpectedly, is not sought, and causes embarrassment. St Teresa of Avila spent hours praying for it to stop and never to return. One of the most well-known examples is St Joseph of Copertino, whose many witnesses included Prince Casimir of Poland, the Spanish ambassador to the Holy See and Frederick Duke of Brunswick, who abjured Lutheranism as a result. If we reject the evidence of people such as these, how shall we ever find any acceptable historical evidence?

The gift of levitation is often accompanied by that of bi-location, as was the case with Don Bosco and, more recently Padre Pio. During the Second World War the American Air Force's General Command was located in Bari and it was from there that the Commanding Officer wanted to lead a squadron of bombers to destroy a depot of German war material that had been stored in the town of St Giovanni Rotondo. The General later described how, when the planes were near their target, he and his men saw in the sky a friar with uplifted hands. The bombs dropped away of their own accord and fell into some woods. As for the aeroplanes, they reversed course without being manoeuvred by the pilots. Everyone aboard was mystified. Later, someone mentioned to the General that in a Capuchin friary in that very town lived a certain friar who had a reputation for holiness. The General decided that, as soon as the war was over, he would go and visit this friary. This he did, in the company of some pilots. After entering and finding himself in the presence of various friars, the General immediately recognized the one who had stopped his aircraft: it was Padre Pio. Pio walked towards him saying kindly, 'Are you the one who wanted to kill us all?' Relieved by these words and by the look on Pio's face, the General fell to his knees. As usual, Pio had spoken to him in dialect; but the General, like so many others, was convinced that he had been spoken to in his own language. The two became friends and the Protestant General converted to Catholicism.

To return to the angels of the Provençal legend, it is undeniably true that many people today – because of the way in which the word has changed meaning in recent centuries – feel that what is 'symbolic' is not real. Yet the traditional depiction of Mary Magdalen as being surrounded or supported by angels points to a basic spiritual truth.

I was reminded of this after reading a second-hand copy of a book by the great French theologian Cardinal Jean Daniélou that I accidentally came across some time after my conversations with Philippe. I doubt whether he has ever read it, but it expresses in more theological terms exactly the point he had made. *Les Anges et leur mission – d'après les Pères de l'Église* made for rewarding reading, especially the chapter on the role of angels in our spiritual life.

Daniélou shows how the Fathers repeatedly stressed that it is by the ministry of the angels that the soul is assisted in its ascent towards God. What could be more natural than to convey this notion of elevation by linking it to the geology and configuration of the Sainte-Baume range itself? The angels are 'real levers', says Gregory of Nyssa in his *Life of Moses*, sent to help raise us to the spiritual heights. Real, yes, but it is not the visible that is the most 'real' aspect of creation.

Will future generations, one wonders, lose all sense of the difference between being 'lifted up' and being 'uplifted'? Will they fail to see the joke in the title of the Flanders and Swann song about the typical London omnibus: 'A Transport of Delight'?

❦

C'est tellement mystérieux, le pays des larmes.
(Saint-Exupéry, *Le Petit Prince*)

In what is perhaps his least superficial role, Gérard Depardieu takes the part of Marin Marais, celebrated seventeenth-century viol player and composer. Based closely on Pascal Quignard's historical fiction *Tous les matins du monde*, Alain Corneau's 1991 film compares him unfavourably with his real-life teacher, Monsieur de Sainte Colombe – a solitary genius who shunned the vulgarity of high society and the royal court.

Sainte Colombe would sing to his two young daughters, the elder of whom was named Madeleine, as they sobbed at night after their mother's unexpected death. Often he would choose the following lines – which summed up his own emotional state as well as that of the girls – from a motet by Marc-Antoine Charpentier, composed in the late seventeenth century as one of his Five Meditations for Lent:

Sola vivebat in antris Magdalena
Lugens et suspirans die ac nocte.

Even the experts are unable to trace the author of the lyrics. Without question, however, they typify what had long ago become the generally accepted view, only to be reinforced in the Jansenist seventeenth century, of what Mary Magdalen spent her time doing in Provence: 'Madeleine lived alone in a cave, mourning and sighing both day and night.'

Nothing about Mary has been more misunderstood than her tears. Her very name has been corrupted into a pejorative adjective that denotes anything excessively and self-pityingly sentimental: *maudlin*. French is a little kinder: *pleurer comme une madeleine* simply means to cry one's heart out. In depicting her, artists have often chosen to exaggerate precisely this feature. It makes for good art but, as so often with western painting since the Renaissance, bad theology. In the Gospel accounts, of course, she does weep. The Greek verb used (κλαίω) can admittedly also mean to 'wail' or 'bemoan'. Yet need not. It is, for example, the same verb that Luke uses in his account of the unnamed sinner. Clearly there is no contextual likelihood that the woman, whether or not she is to be identified with Mary Magdalen, was on that occasion wailing.

Yet if, during the final ascetic years of her life, Mary did weep, how are we to interpret her tears? It is not enough simply to classify them as tears of repentance, for repentance too has often been misunderstood. Indeed, I have several times heard it played down by pilgrims. Why, the argument goes, should she want to spend such a long time in repentance? Did she not truly believe that Christ had forgiven her sins? Such a line of reasoning is probably part and parcel of a more widespread loss of awareness of the true meaning of spiritual mourning.

To begin with, it is clear that for Mary Magdalen the situation was altered radically by her privileged meeting with the risen Jesus. The same positive conviction that, according to the Provençal legend itself, caused her to proclaim the good news must surely remove from the equation any ideas of lugubrious lamentation. In fact, according to Mark (16:10), it is the disciples who 'mourned and wept', not Mary, as she rushed to tell them her wonderful news. The immediate followers of Jesus were empowered not by Calvary but by the Resurrection and by Pentecost. The fondness of artists for depicting a grief-stricken Mary, along with a literary tradition typified on this side of the Channel by Southwell's sixteenth-century melodramatic prose meditation entitled *Mary Magdalen's Funeral Tears*, have combined to elevate the funereal aspect out of all proportion. Yet any post-Resurrection tears shed in the Sainte Baume would have had nothing in common with those of Margery Kempe, the fifteenth-century so-called mystic who identified herself with Mary (or, rather, with her own image of her) and who became a social nuisance with her great sobbings and sighings, her loud weeping, wailing and screaming.

But there is more to it than that.

It seems that tears are a uniquely human phenomenon. Medical textbooks tell us that there are two main causes: emotional (positive or negative) and physical (as when we are in great pain or when an irritant has affected our eyes). In both cases the liquid is chemically different from our ordinary eye lubricant. Moreover, tears flush out minerals and hormones related to stress and depression. In short, they are good for us. In America they are now even regarded as the new Prozac.

However, for true Christian ascetics the tears that really count – and they are far from being a specifically feminine phenomenon – are neither physical nor emotional but spiritual, in the sense of being a gift of the Holy Spirit. Yet it is precisely these that those who write on Mary Magdalen from a historical, socio-cultural point of view seem ill-equipped to discuss.

Perhaps Mary Magdalen did indeed withdraw into the Sainte Baume to lead a life of asceticism which involved the shedding of tears. Yet, as most spiritual masters stress, great care and discernment are required in order to distinguish between the many occasions and types. Nor ought tears be squeezed out, for this amounts only to the weeping of the outward man. Genuinely spiritual tears come unexpectedly, unbidden. They overflow gently – as a wound 'weeps' – from 'the deep waters of the heart' (Wisdom 2:2), 'heart' being understood in its biblical sense as the spiritual rather than emotional centre of man's being. They flow amid silence. There is no sobbing; there are no facial contortions.

Mary's tears, then, should not be thought of as a negative, gloomy manifestation. Nonetheless, they would have coexisted with a deep feeling of sorrow. Yet such compunction (κατάνυξις or *compunctio cordis*) is likewise far from being a negative condition; it is inextricably mingled with tenderness and joy. John Climacus, Desert Father (*c.* 570–649) and Abbot of Sinai, has an entire chapter in his *Ladder of Divine Ascent* entitled 'On Joyful Mourning'. In our own days, Cardinal Jean Daniélou pointed out in another of his books, *Jean-Baptiste, témoin de l'Agneau,* that 'les plus grands pénitents sont les plus grands joyeux'. It is in fact this feature that is a test of whether tears are genuinely spiritual. For deep repentance produces a consciousness not merely of one's sins but also, more importantly, of God's loving forgiveness.

Thus, repentance is not to be equated, as it often is, with 'doing penance', a legalistic concept, with negative connotations. The Greek word for it (μετάνοια) primarily signifies not just regret or self-reproach but, more importantly and more fundamentally, a 'change of mind', a positive turning of our whole life towards God. This positive slant is what causes John Climacus (in Step 5 of *The Ladder*) to write that 'Repentance is the daughter of hope'. He doesn't say 'mother', but 'daughter'.

All the same, to return to the objection stated earlier, why should Mary have spent so many years repenting for her sins at all? Had they not been forgiven?

To answer this, we must first remember that it is those closest to God who are most conscious of their unworthiness. It is precisely those who, like Isaiah (6:5), have had a vision of him who are most likely to cry out, 'Woe is me!' Those closest to the light see the most specks of dust.

Secondly, as the Desert Fathers also stressed, 'sin' is a

question not simply of one's own individual sinful acts or thoughts. That is what occupies the beginner. Even should he progress to sorrow for those of others, whether personally known to him or not, there is yet another stage to be reached. Namely, the realisation that, first and foremost, 'sin' denotes a state, a permanent fallen condition affecting not just ourselves or others including newly born babies, but creation in its entirety. As Paul says in Romans, 'the whole creation has been groaning in travail together until now' (8:22).

It is to this condition that John is referring (1:29) when he speaks of the Lamb of God who takes away 'the *sin* of the world'. Unfortunately, the use of the plural (*qui tollis peccata mundi*) in the *Agnus Dei* and the *Gloria*, heard weekly or even daily down the centuries, has all but removed this from our awareness.

When we become truly aware of our exile from Paradise, how can we not – like the Jewish exiles in Babylon (Psalm 137) – occasionally sit down and weep? How can we not experience an abiding sense of sorrow for sin? It is no accident that in Syriac one word for a monk is *abila*, a 'mourner'. '*Blessed are they who mourn, for they shall be comforted.* But the mourning for which [the Lord] promises eternal consolation,' says Leo the Great in a Sermon on the Beatitudes, 'has nothing to do with ordinary worldly distress; for the tears which have their origin in the sorrow common to all mankind do not make anyone blessed.'

Properly understood, then, repentance – like salvation itself – is a lifelong process lasting till death and beyond. The deathbed words of another Egyptian Desert Father, Abba Sisoes, make this clear: 'See,' he said to his disciples, 'the angels have come to take me and I am asking for a little more time – more time to repent.' 'You have no need to repent,' said his disciples. 'Truly,' he replied, 'I am not sure whether I have even begun to repent.' Likewise, one of the petitions in the litanies which punctuate the Byzantine Liturgy is 'that we may spend the rest of our lives in peace and repentance'. The link with peace is deliberate; for this, rather than an agonizing negativity, is what true repentance – the kind we must surely associate with Mary Magdalen – ultimately induces.

The answer, then, to the objection I had encountered is not that she repents in order to be forgiven. She has indeed already been forgiven. Her repentance is a consequence, the result of an ever-deepening insight into the merciful love of Christ. The closer we come to him, the more we feel the need to repent.

❧

... clothed in naught but thy long hair.

For obvious reasons, the above aspect of the legend, particularly when represented visually, is one that occasions considerable interest. Before discussing its veracity and origin, let us first allow ourselves a slight deviation by way of François Villon.

In his *Ballade pour prier Notre Dame,* part of his *Testament* (*c.* 1461–2), Villon has the following lines:

A vostre Filz dictes que je suis sienne;
De lui soyent mes pechiez absolus;
Pardonne moy comme a l'Egipcienne.

Tell your Son that I am his;
May he pardon me and forgive my sins;
As he did those of the Egyptian woman.

Who is this Egyptian woman, whom Villon assumes to be so familiar to his readers that he need not name her? Moreover, why introduce her to our investigation of the Provençal legend? Precisely because it is believed that certain details of her story became attached to that of Mary Magdalen, including her nakedness.

The story of Mary of Egypt was extremely popular in the Middle Ages. Hildebert, Archbishop of Tours – a celebrated poet and hymnologist – had done a version in Latin verse at the beginning of the twelfth century. Jehan de Reims had already attempted the task. But it was Rutebeuf's thirteenth-century French verse version, along with Voragine's Latin prose version (soon translated) that gave definitive popularity to the tale in France. The version of Rutebeuf – the 'Minstrel of Paris' – was, in fact, a reworking of an earlier anonymous poem, which must have been widespread since it exists in several manuscripts concerning lives of saints.

It is a little-known fact that the unassuming Rue de la Jussienne in Paris, situated behind the Hôtel des Postes, refers to this saint. It takes its name from the church dedicated to her, Sainte Marie l'Égyptienne, which was erected here. Over the centuries the name became misunderstood and deformed, particularly after the church's demolition during the Revolution. *L'Égyptienne* became *la Gyptienne* and finally *la Jussienne*, the version which survives in the name of the street to this day.

The oldest archival reference to the church dates from 1372. However, it was erected a good hundred years earlier on the wishes of Louis IX, St Louis. The king had heard the story of the saint during his crusade in the Holy Land. Full of admiration, he decided to build a church in her honour and, as a further sign of the importance he attached to her life and message, chose a site quite near the Louvre.

Yet this was not the first time news of Mary had reached France.

According to the Bollandists, a group of erudite Jesuits who since the seventeenth century have specialized in editing a multi-volumed critical edition (*Acta Sanctorum*) of the lives of saints, the oldest written mention of her in France seems to have been in the *Life of Saint Marius* written in 601 by Dynamius. (Marius was abbot of the now destroyed monastery of Bodon, north of Nyons in the Drôme; the village of St-May preserves the memory of his name in its Provençal form.) The text contains a reference to a lion 'which dug out the graves of St Paul the Hermit

[...] and also of Mary of Egypt'. Based at Marseilles, Dynamius was Governor of Provence from 575 to 587. He is mentioned in Gregory of Tours' *History of the Franks* (Book 6) and in the correspondence of Gregory the Great. Towards the end of his life, he founded a monastery in the locality and withdrew from the world, writing several saints' lives. We must assume from this that Mary's story was known in Provence as least as early as the late sixth century.

The oldest Greek text of the complete story is generally believed to be the work of Sophronius (*c.* 560-638), who had been a monk in Egypt and Palestine before being elected Patriarch in 635. However, the Bollandists say it was written before 500. Whoever the original author was, he simply uses an anonymous first-person in his Prologue and Epilogue. It is in reading them that we learn that he considered the story so valuable that it needed to be set down in writing. As the text states, he based his version on the oral tradition which he heard at first hand in the monastery which features in the tale. This was the monastery where a certain Zosimas lived, the one who discovered the saint far off in the Jordanian desert and who, after her death, recounted the events connected with her.

'The monks preserved this story without writing it down,' we read in the Epilogue. 'Nobody has heard of anyone writing it down to this day; but I have told in writing what I heard orally. Perhaps others have also described the life of the saint [...] although this has not come to my notice.'

Clearly, Sophronius was simply sanctioning, by means of a literary text, a cult which had long existed.

❧

St Mary the Egyptian is one of the great spiritual athletes of Christendom and a model of the ascetic life. As such, it is not difficult to see why aspects of her story should have been merged at an early date with that of the Provençal

Mary Magdalen, particularly since both shared the same Christian name. Her exact dates are difficult to state with exactitude, though she was probably born around the year 344 and died in about 421.

As a young teenager she left her home for Alexandria where for more than seventeen years she led a life of public prostitution. She tells us that she was more interested in the pleasure than the money. On the occasion of a pilgrimage to Jerusalem for the Feast of the Exaltation of the Cross, she embarked for Palestine. Not as a pilgrim but in the hope that on board she would find many new clients and occasions to satisfy her lust. Once in Jerusalem she joined the crowds going towards the church of the Holy Sepulchre. When she tried to enter, an invisible force thrust her back. Having tried unsuccessfully three or four times, she withdrew, perturbed by the mysterious power that was impeding her. But not before she had caught sight of an icon of the Mother of God above the spot where she had been standing.

Suddenly struck with remorse for her wicked life, she spent the night in prayer and tears. Next morning she found she could enter the church without hindrance. After venerating the Cross, she left Jerusalem and crossed the Jordan, settling as a solitary in a remote area of the desert. Here she lived for forty-seven years undetected until found by a priest-monk named Zosimas.

As was the custom in several monasteries in Egypt and Palestine, at the start of Lent Zosimas had gone out into the desert to live a life of seclusion, in imitation of Christ's forty-day retreat. He would return in time for Palm Sunday. However, on one occasion he spotted an emaciated, naked creature who turned out to be Mary. Eventually she told him her story. Of how her clothes had eventually rotted away and of how she had survived on roots and herbs. She made him promise to return the following year on the evening of Holy Thursday and to bring her communion. It would be the first time she had communicated since leaving Jerusalem forty-seven years earlier.

At the appointed time, he waited for her, as agreed, on the west bank of the Jordan. When she eventually appeared on the other side, he was amazed to see that she was able to join him by walking across the river. A year later, he returned to the original place of their meeting only to find that she had died. In the earth by her body, she had traced her name and the fact that she had passed away on Good Friday, the day after receiving communion.

Is her story historical? Before we dismiss it in its entirety, it is worth pointing out that in 1890 the Greek priest Joachim Spetsieris wrote a true account (*I erimitis Photeini eis tin eremou tou Iordanou*) of having found a woman hermit, named Photini, in the desert beyond the Jordan, living in much the same way as Mary must have done. (A recent English translation exists, entitled *The Hermitess Photini.*) Moreover, even in our own lifetime a few hermits on Mount Athos go naked, eating grass and herbs, living among the animals. Jacques Valentin, in his 1960 book *The Monks of Mount Athos*, tells how he himself saw one at fairly close quarters.

Yet our immediate concern is the influence the story of Mary of Egypt may have had on the Provençal tradition. Her nakedness, obviously. Her former life as a prostitute. Though not her hair. For in the standard text, the one attributed to Sophronius, this is unambiguously described as being 'white as wool and not long, coming down no lower than the neck'. It is as if the narrator is making the point that her hair, too, had been affected by her life of severe asceticism. Icons of the saint likewise always depict her with short hair.

From where, then, was the body-length hair motif borrowed?

In the first place, the Gospel passages in which Mary wipes Jesus' feet with her hair imply that it must have been longer rather than shorter. Yet there was nothing unusual in this. What was striking was that the woman had let her hair down in public. Secondly, we have seen how in Provence Mary had to some extent replaced Diana (or

Artemis), the Ephesian goddess who in turn had absorbed several of the attributes of Cybele. It may be relevant that this name has been thought – at least, until recently – to mean 'she of the hair'. Moreover, an extremely common representation showed her, not simply as many-breasted, but with body and legs enclosed within a tapering pillar-like so-called *term*, from which her feet protrude. An example can be seen in the *Musée d'Archéologie Mediterranéenne* at Marseilles. It is possible that this was adapted as all-enclosing hair.

A third possibility is a later Greek version of a tale similar to Mary of Egypt's – never, apparently, translated into Latin – of which Benedicta Ward gives an extract in her *Harlots of the Desert*. This story concerns a nun, rather than a prostitute, who broke her vows of chastity in Jerusalem, not Alexandria, and who is not named. Nevertheless, like Mary, she retires to a life of solitude in the desert. More relevant is the fact that she not only lived in a cave but that, after her clothes wore out, her hair grew to such an extent that she was entirely covered with it.

None of these possible sources are, of course, mutually exclusive. This question of influences is something I shall return to later, when considering whether it is possible to unearth the original story of Mary Magdalen in Provence. First, however, we must examine the case of someone else familiar with the ascetic life in Palestine and Egypt. Someone whose dates are roughly contemporary with those of Mary of Egypt and who quite possibly had heard of her story, if only in the oral version. Someone, moreover, who definitely did come to Provence and whose influence there, as in the West in general, has been unfairly eclipsed.

5

Desert Spirituality Comes to Provence

Studying any detailed map of this part of Provence, you soon become aware that a certain name seems to crop up time and again: Cassien. Over to the East in the Estérel massif, twenty kilometres from Cannes, is the Lac St-Cassien. Among anglers this is perhaps the most legendary lake in Europe; carp weighing over thirty kilos have been caught. Yet it is a relatively recent creation, dating from the 1960s. However, at its north-eastern extremity is the Barrage de St-Cassien and, just beyond this, the Chapelle St-Cassien. This medieval chapel also used to be called St Cassien-des-Bois; presumably to distinguish it from the Ermitage de St-Cassien, sometimes known as the Butte St-Cassien, which now finds itself a stone's throw from Cannes' small airport.

An abbot from the nearby island of Saint-Honorat built a hermitage here in the seventh century in a grove which had been the site of a pagan temple. It was rebuilt in the Middle Ages. Since Cassien is also the patron saint of Cannes, it is in and around the chapel on this Butte, or hillock, on his feast day in July that Mass is celebrated, followed by an open-air meal and a *bal champêtre*.

In the Sainte-Baume region itself, to return to our particular focus of interest, the same name is also frequently found. At the eastern tip of the range, there is the Baou or Pic de St-Cassien on which is erected La Croix de St-

Cassien. Not far from the cave associated with Mary Magdalen can be found Le Petit St-Cassien, an old cluster of buildings, the Aven (or sinkhole) du Petit St-Cassien, and Le Grand St-Cassien, which seems to be a ruined hermitage. In the nineteenth century, according to Lacordaire, local shepherds spoke of a spring which they called the Source St-Cassien, though they didn't know why.

Who is this 'Cassien' and what is his relationship with the region? Since he is believed to have had a direct influence on the tradition we are investigating, these are questions worth asking.

John Cassian died in 435, having been born in approximately 360, though exactly where is a matter of debate, as we shall see. When still a young man, he had set off for Palestine with an older friend, Germanus, in search of a living tradition of monasticism. The two were received into a monastery in Bethlehem where they spent seven years. Still unsatisfied, they longed to travel to the Nile Delta in Egypt where monasticism had started in the third century and where the most revered anchorites and spiritual masters were still to be found. They were to spend fifteen years here, with Scete in the Nitrian desert as their base.

They then went to Constantinople, the great centre of Byzantine Christianity. There John was made deacon by St John Chrysostom, John the Golden-Mouthed, so called because of the effectiveness of his preaching. According to Palladius – in his biography of Chrysostom, of whom he was a friend and supporter – Cassian seems to have been put in charge of the treasury of Hagia Sophia. When Chrysostom was deposed because of his criticism of the Emperor's morals, Cassian was delegated to take to Pope Innocent I a request for support from the pro-Chrysostom clergy. It was in Rome that he is thought to have been ordained priest.

It seems to have been around the time that Alaric was laying siege to Rome (408–10) that John left for Marseilles. Why he should have opted for this destination is not clear. Some say he was returning to his homeland. Others say he was invited by the monastically inclined Bishop of Marseilles, Proculus (381–428).

In all, he had spent some twenty-five years in the Middle East. A few monasteries had already been founded in France, most notably those of St Martin and St Hilary of Poitiers at Ligugé and Tours and the recent one on the Iles de Lérins, off Cannes. On the whole, however, after his long experience of the original tradition, John found this fledgling monasticism to be poorly organized, undisciplined and heavily dependent on the personality of the founders or present leaders. Not enough attention was paid to asceticism, the inner life, or the perfection of the heart. Cassian also believed that monks should be self-supporting and was surprised to find that in Gaul this did not seem to be universally the case.

He spent the last twenty years of his life in Marseilles – where he wrote his two most famous books, the *Institutes* and the *Conferences* – and the surrounding area. He founded two monasteries in the city: one for women (Saint-Sauveur) and the more famous one for men (Saint-Victor) which, rebuilt several times, survives to this day. It was so named because it was built over the tomb of this converted soldier, who was martyred under Maximian around 310. The site had originally been a quarry and then a Christian necropolis, clustered round the tombs of two earlier martyrs who perished under Decius *c.* 250.

However, if the average western Christian has heard of John Cassian at all, it is likely to be as the originator of what has been known since the seventeenth century as Semi-Pelagianism.

Pelagius maintained that man could achieve salvation by his own efforts and moral discipline. In his polemic against him (410–20), Augustine had stressed the absolute need for grace. To the monks of Provence this line of reasoning failed to do justice to the human element, to man's free will. It was, moreover, a dangerously novel view that seemed to ignore biblical teaching. Indeed, its effects down the ages can be seen in such typically western controversies as those surrounding the notions of grace and free will: Calvinism, predestination, Jansenism, Molinism and the like. Moreover, Cassian had studied in an environment in which Greek theologians had had to deal not with a Pelagian excessive optimism, but a pagan oriental fatalism.

Cassian himself took no personal part in the controversy. The trouble began when Prosper of Aquitaine, an over-enthusiastic admirer of Augustine's writings on grace and predestination, took exception to what he claimed to be Cassian's teaching. He attempted to enlist Augustine's support, writing to him that monks in the area of Marseilles were expressing alternative views. After Augustine's death, Prosper even tried to elicit a papal condemnation. This proved unsuccessful. Not least because, as a trusted Greek-speaking friend of Archdeacon Leo (himself a future Pope), Cassian had just been persuaded by Leo to compose for the same Pope (Celestine) an anti-Nestorian treatise entitled *On the Incarnation of the Lord*. Significantly, in this he linked the wayward Nestorius to none other than Pelagius. Prosper continued his attacks, however, publishing a critique of Cassian's Conference 13, which he claimed contained clear evidence of Cassian's errors. Things rumbled on until, long after Cassian's death, the Second Council of Orange (529) – undoubtedly influenced by Prosper's version of the Augustinian and Cassianite views – condemned the teaching of Bishop Faustus of Riez, who was still maintaining a pro-Cassian position.

Ironically, it is this position which represents the traditional view that, after the Fall, man may not be sound (as in the Pelagian view), yet nor is he dead (as strict Augustinians argued). Rather, he is sick, retaining some vestige of his created goodness. Cassian was simply passing on in a balanced and spiritually mature fashion the teachings of the Eastern Fathers. (Augustine himself knew hardly any Greek.) Augustine's last writings on the matter, addressed to Prosper – *On The Predestination of the Saints* and *The Gift of Perseverance* – reveal a polemical hardening. He seems even to deny that salvation is for all. Whether or not one is elected becomes ultimately arbitrary. This is a view that Augustine's mentor Ambrose would hardly have recognized. It does not even harmonize with Augustine's own earlier teaching.

It is difficult to understand why Cassian should ever have been accused of heresy. To begin with, his view – the standard view among the Greek Fathers – that the sinner is not dead but sick agrees with Christ's own rebuttal when criticized for eating with 'sinners': 'They that are whole need not a physician, but they that are sick' (Matthew 9:12). Indeed it agrees with the 1992 Catechism (§ 405), which describes fallen human nature as 'wounded'. Of course, no doctor can help a patient who does not *want* to be healed. This too fits with Christ's own admiration for those who approached him with faith. Similarly, in Matthew's Gospel Jesus affirms, 'knock, and it will be opened to you' (7:7). The door does not open until we knock. In Revelation, John uses the same image but from the opposite point of view: 'I stand at the door and knock,' Christ says; 'if anyone hears my voice and opens the door, I will come in to him' (3:20). God knocks, but we are left free to decide whether or not we will open the door. Paul conveys this co-operation between divine grace and human freedom by describing us as 'fellow-workers [συνεργοί] with God' (1 Corinthians 3:9). God's part is immeasurably greater, yet it does not rule out our own contribution. He may be all-powerful; but his power is one of love, one that respects the freedom of the beloved. Indeed, it is surely a tenet of the faith that, at that crucial turning point in the history of salvation called the Annunciation, Mary's free will was likewise respected. Gabriel does not depart until she has freely given her response.

The orthodoxy of Cassian's position is further seen in the way it conforms to recent pronouncements by Cardinal Arinze, Prefect of the Congregation for Divine Worship, made when explaining the Vatican's decision to reinstate in the prayer of consecration the phrase 'for many', as opposed to the parvenu 'for all'. The former is, of course, the phrase used by Jesus in the Gospels; but Cardinal Arinze chose to stress a different reason for the decision. He explained that *pro multis* reflects the fact that salvation is not brought about in some mechanical way 'without one's own willingness or participation'.

Reading Cassian's Conference 13 for oneself – and like all his work it contains an impressive array of biblical quotes – it is obvious that Prosper's account of it is nothing less than a travesty. Cassian is accused of teaching that the initial impulse for good comes from ourselves alone and precedes grace. Yet it is precisely this error that the entire conference is designed to correct! The introductory chapter could not be more clear: 'man even though he strive with all his might for a good result, yet cannot become master of what is good unless he has acquired it simply by the gift of Divine bounty and not by the efforts of his own toil'. Similarly, in Chapter 3 we read that 'the *initiative* not only of our actions but also of good thoughts comes from God'. The chapter headings are themselves eminently orthodox: On the Weakness of the Will (Ch.10); How Human Efforts Cannot be Set Against the Grace of God (Ch. 13); The Decision of the Fathers that Free Will is not Equal to Save a Man (Ch. 18).

To anyone trained in the East, Augustine's approach – or, more accurately, the use to which it was put – would have seemed like logical hair-splitting, far removed from lived spirituality. The sort of approach, in fact, that Cassian had warned against in the closing pages of Conference 13: 'empty disputes of words' (Ch. 18). God's grace, though primary, works in harmony with human freedom. Precisely how and in what proportions, it is pointless to speculate. For, quoting Paul again, he stresses that '[God's] ways are past finding out' (Ch. 15). We should fight against 'any more subtle inference of man's argumentation and reasoning', whilst accepting that the 'desire of everything that is good' is itself 'a Divine gift' (Ch. 18).

In short, Cassian's position should not be interpreted pejoratively as Semi-Pelagian, but as a positive attempt to steer a moderate course between the two extremes of Pelagianism and hard-line Augustinianism. As for Augustine, it is in such works as his sermons rather than his polemical writings that he is often most balanced and at his best. In Sermon 169, for example, which could have been written by Cassian himself: 'For He who made you without your consent [*sine te*] will not justify you without your consent.'

❦

The suspicion that has unfairly dogged Cassian has meant that, though his influence has been pervasive, he has never been formally canonized in the West. In the Greek and other Orthodox Churches, on the other hand, St John Cassian is additionally honoured by being the only Latin writer to have been included (in translation) in the prestigious compilations known as the *Sayings of the Desert Fathers* and *The Philokalia*, the normative collection of texts written between the fourth and fifteenth centuries by the spiritual masters of the Orthodox tradition. This alone is proof that he was himself considered to be a Desert Father and that, despite his extreme modesty, his writings are the fruit of someone who speaks with psychological finesse from his own mature experience and not – despite the format of the *Conferences* – merely the notes of a scribe passing on the conversations and sayings of others, gathered many years previously. Moreover, in the Marseilles area and more widely in Provence, he is likewise considered a saint. His tomb, situated in the crypt of Saint-Victor, was venerated until despoiled at the Revolution. It is reported that Urban V, perhaps the best of the Avignon popes and a former abbot of Saint-Victor, had the words 'Saint Cassian' engraved on the silver casket that contained his skull.

We have already seen that the anti-Pelagian Pope Leo the Great thought very highly of the older man, ever since meeting him in Rome. Cassian's warm words about Leo in the preface to his *On the Incarnation* testify to their friendship. Pope Gelasius (d.496), conversely, was once believed to have further censored Cassian in *De libris recipiendis*

(*Books to be Received*); but this is now known to be a sixth-century non-papal private compilation. In any case, it had little effect so far as Cassian's writings were concerned.

In 512 St Caesarius, Bishop of Arles, founded a convent there, persuading his own sister (Caesaria) to leave Cassian's foundation of Saint-Sauveur at Marseilles in order to be its first abbess. His celebrated rule for women owed much to Cassian's writings. The monastically inclined Gregory the Great (d.604) – the first monk, in fact, to be elected Pope – certainly considered him to be a saint and was much influenced by him. In his Epistle 12 of *Book 7* – addressed to Respecta, Abbess of Massilia – he refers to 'the monastery [=convent] consecrated to the honour of Saint Cassian wherein you are selected to preside'. It was from Cassian that Gregory adopted and introduced (in a somewhat simplified form) what became known in the West as the Seven Deadly Sins.

The influence is even more pronounced in the case of St Benedict (d.550), whose Rule owes much to Cassian and quotes him at length. His own Rule, he says in its closing chapter, is for beginners; those who wish to make further progress should read the two works by Cassian. Benedict described the *Conferences* as being a 'mirror of monasticism' and said that the book should be read daily by his monks. Indeed it was its regular reading in the refectory during the evening meal which caused this sort of light meal to become known as a 'collation', from the Latin title of Cassian's text: *Collationes*.

Cassian's popularity continued unabated. St Bruno, who founded the Carthusian order in 1084, also thought very highly of his writings. St Dominic recommended daily perusal of the *Conferences* and they seem to have been the favourite reading material of Thomas Aquinas.

St Bernard, too, was much influenced by Cassian's writings. By his time, the original Benedictine tradition, particularly at Cluny, had been to some extent watered down. It was this that motivated him to seek a return to the primitive ideal, which in effect meant a return to the ideal, among others, of Cassian. In his book on Cassian, Chadwick rightly points out that 'Saint Bernard and the Cistercians, with their simplicity and their affection for the direct and prayerful experience of the mystics, laid far more weight upon those ideals which were represented in the inheritance of Egypt. The Rule never lost its [final] seventy-third chapter; and its seventy-third chapter continued to remind the Benedictines of Egypt and of Cassian.' The following extract from Bernard's *De gratia et libero arbitrio* might well have been penned by the supposedly Semi-Pelagian himself: 'Remove free will, and there is nothing to be saved; remove grace, and there is left no means of saving. The work of salvation cannot be accomplished without the co-operation of the two.'

The immense number of manuscripts of his writings which proliferated throughout the Middle Ages are in themselves evidence of the high esteem in which Cassian was held.

In his own day Cassian's reputation, even before he had written a single line, must have spread quickly. For not many years after the foundation of Saint-Victor, he was asked to set down for others the fruits of his experiences in the East. The request for the *Institutes* (*c.* 420) came from Bishop Castor of Apta Julia (Apt), a town some forty miles north of Marseilles. This is explicitly stated in the Preface, where Cassian describes Castor as being 'anxious that the institutions of the East and especially of Egypt should be established in [his] province, which is at present without monasteries'. Cleary, Castor considered Cassian to be not only an authoritative living witness of the original desert tradition but a sure guide for the new monastery he was founding at Ménerbes.

The second of his two monastic classics, the *Conferences*, was also composed as a result of a request from Castor. The first book had a section on remedies for the eight 'obstacles' that a monk would have to surmount. (It was from these that Gregory the Great composed his list, referred to earlier, of Seven Deadly Sins.) It was mainly concerned, however, with the organization of the monastic life, with rules for the outer man. On the other hand, the *Conferences* – so called because composed as a series of 'interviews' with the Desert Fathers who, as it were, speak to us directly – were more concerned with the training of the inner man and the interior life.

Since Castor had unexpectedly died by the time the first group was completed, Cassian dedicated them instead to Léontius, Bishop of Fréjus and Castor's brother. The middle group of Conferences were dedicated to Honoratus, who had been ordained by Léontius. St Honoratus was the founder (*c.* 410) of the important monastery on the smaller of a group of two islands – the Iles de Lérins – off Cannes. It is today called Saint-Honorat after him. Of the young monasteries in France, this was the one of which Cassian most approved. Like Cassian, Honoratus had set off to visit the eastern Desert Fathers. However, after the death in Greece of his brother and companion, he decided to return to Provence. It is easy to imagine the rapport that must have existed between the two men and to understand how eagerly Honoratus would have welcomed a first-hand account of the teachings of the very spiritual masters he himself had so wanted to learn from.

A slightly later abbot of Lérins, Faustus, became Bishop of Riez in upper Provence in 459. It was he whose *De Gratia*, written at the request of the Archbishop of Arles to counter continuing unyieldingly predestinarian tendencies, was criticized some seventy years later at Orange. Yet even such a staunchly pro-Augustinian advocate as the North African Bishop Fulgentius (died *c.* 527), who composed a book attacking Faustus, nevertheless admired Cassian's writings to such an extent that he too attempted (unsuccessfully) to visit Egypt.

The final group of Conferences is dedicated to four monks who had established a community on one of the islands off Hyères. Theodore, singled out for praise, later became the successor of Léontius as Bishop of Fréjus.

All in all, despite misunderstandings of his teaching, it is clear that in his own day (as afterwards) Cassian was highly regarded as a wise authority. Judiciously combining community life with that of the solitary, with great discernment he transmitted to Provence and thus to the West in general the best of the original 'desert spirituality'. The importance of his role cannot be overstated. In the twenty-first century, his writings are as fresh, as sound and as relevant as ever.

❧

St John Cassian's feast day in Provence falls on 23 July, the day after that of Mary Magdalen. Is this accidental, or an indication of a deeper connection between the two? Certainly there is much that would seem to link him and his followers with the region of the Sainte-Baume, as our opening discussion of place-names suggests.

We must return to the debate surrounding his origins.

Until relatively recently it was commonly held that Cassian was indeed born in the vicinity of Marseilles, a true son of Provence. All rests on a brief allusion by the ecclesiastical historian Gennadius of Marseilles. In his *De Viris Illustribus* (AD 480), written some forty-five years after John Cassian's death, he refers to him as being 'natione Scytha'. For long, it was assumed that the phrase referred to the desert of Scete (or Scetis) in Egypt, where Cassian spent many years of his life and with which place his reputation was associated. The full, original title of his *Conferences* includes this reference: *Collationes Patrum in Scithio Eremo Commorantium.*

One local historian, Marius Frezet, claimed that Gennadius' handwriting must have been poor, since in some copies the key phrase appears as *in Cirtha* or *in Serda*. The original text, in his view, read *in Cytharista*; that is, La Ciotat, just along the coast from Marseilles.

However, in 1945 Henri Marrou put forward the view that Cassian came from Scythia Minor, a part of the Empire situated in what is nowadays Dobrogea (Dobruja) in

Romania. It is certainly the case that a community of monks – the so-called 'Scythian monks' – were active there from the fourth to the sixth century. One of their number, before he moved to Rome, was Denis the Little, inventor of the Anno Domini system of dating.

Most have been convinced. Some feel that the traditional case for a Provençal origin still stands. They reply that the word *Cassiani* may well have been found in Romania on an early inscription, but that the name was very common in both the western and eastern halves of the Empire. For example, an early bishop of Autun was named Cassian. Born in Alexandria, he died in Autun in 334. Further west, and at an even earlier date, there is a strong tradition of a Cassian in Tangiers, martyred there in 298. (Interestingly, Victor Gélu – the nineteenth-century bard from Marseilles who wrote in the old local Provençal patois – entitled his most famous ballad *Lou Crèdo dé Cassian*, Cassian being a wise old shepherd.) Those in favour of a Provençal origin also point to the decree issued by Byzantine Emperor Arcadius on 29 August 404. This not only exiled Patriarch John Chrysostom, Cassian's mentor, but also states that his supporters should return 'to their own countries'. We then find Cassian travelling, not north to Scythia, but west to Provence, after an extended stopover in Rome. Others point to the reference in the *Institutes* (11.18) to Cassian's 'own sister'. If, as is believed, he entrusted to her the direction of the convent he established in Marseilles on the hill now known as Notre Dame de la Garde, how did she come to be here, if it was not her home territory?

Antoine de Ruffi's 1696 *Histoire de Marseille* relates that Holstensius, Librarian of the Vatican, states categorically that Cassian was French, basing his opinion on Cassian's own writings. In Chapter 1 of Conference 24, he points out, Cassian expresses the wish *ad repentendam provinicіam atque revisendum parentis* – 'to return to our country and revisit our kinsfolk', as it is normally translated. However, Riffi takes the word 'provinciam' literally, as referring to the Roman province par excellence: Provence. Holstensius also argues that Cassian's Latin style conforms to the way the language was used by other contemporary southern French ecclesiastical writers, such as Vincent of Lérins or Eucher (Eucherius), Bishop of Lyons.

Canon Léon Christiani, in his recently reprinted 1946 study of Cassian, supports this view. Writing one year after Marrou's article was published, he points out that the case for a Provençal origin, far from being a recent thesis, was accepted not only by sixteenth- and seventeenth-century scholars but also by more recent specialists such as '[Jean-Jacques] Ampère, [François] Guizot, Dom Besse [who is credited with having converted Huysmans], Abel, Grützmacher, Pergoire and Dom Pichéry'. (The latter was the editor of the standard 1955 Latin/French edition of Cassian's *Conferences*.)

In his 1961 book on Cassian, Jean-Claude Guy, while accepting a Romanian origin, suggests that the very name 'Cassian' has been misunderstood. It is not, he argues, a family name, but one that refers to a certain district. We should, he concludes, really call him 'John the Cassian'. It is not clear to me, though, how this squares with the names of the two saints mentioned earlier: Cassian of Tangiers and Cassian of Autun.

In fact, it is impossible to arrive at any irrefutable conclusion. In any case, for our present investigation, what is important is not where John Cassian originated; but where he ended up. Of that there is no doubt: Marseilles. Yet, is it possible to establish a Cassianite presence outside the city, in the hills and valleys of the Var? This we need to do, if we wish to say anything more specific about his contribution, if any, to the legend of Mary Magdalen.

❧

Climbing up to the cave, as you emerge from the forest and come to the stone steps, you might reflect that it was Cassianite monks who are believed to have carved out the first primitive version of these. Interestingly, if only symbolically, Conference 16 speaks of retreating 'into the high mountain of solitude'.

Most writers agree with Albanès' documentary evidence, given in his *Le Couvent Royal de Saint-Maximin* (1880), that from the beginning of the fifth century, monks were sent out from Cassian's foundation of Saint-Victor in Marseilles into the surrounding countryside. However, it would not have been to the cave that any Cassianites came first of all. Rather, they began by establishing themselves down on the plain around what was believed to be the tomb of Mary Magdalen. (It is important to remember that there was at that time no major settlement there.) Certainly, the number of known ancient ruined hermitages and monastic settlements in this part of Provence is quite remarkable.

The ex-Benedictine Carthusian monastery at Montrieux, the one associated with Petrarch and his brother, was originally a Cassianite foundation. Just outside Brignoles (some 15km east of Saint-Maximin) is La Celle. Here was established a very early (fifth-century) Cassianite foundation. In the other direction, 10km west of Saint-Maximin, overlooking the small town of Trets, is another fifth-century Cassianite hermitage, Saint Jean-du-Puy. Seriously damaged in the ninth-century Saracen invasions, it was rebuilt in the tenth and reoccupied by Cassianites. After several leases of life, it only ceased to function permanently in 1896. It was here that a certain St Ser was trained, having been attracted from his native Lyons to Provence in the fifth century by John Cassian's reputation. He too seems eventually to have opted for the life of a hermit. His hermitage can be seen in a cave halfway up Mont Sainte-Victoire

Many villages have names which seem to derive from such local saintly hermits, though their history has been lost. For example, St Zacharie (near the Sainte-Baume) and St Clair (near St Jean de Garguier). Then there is the sixth-century St Quinis, who later became Bishop of Vaison, but whose hermitage overlooked Besse-sur-Issole.

Since Saint-Victor is believed – again according to Albanès – to have produced at its apogee some 5,000 monks, there must be many more sites and hermitages yet to be discovered. For the time being, it is clear that enough evidence exists of an early, pervasive Cassianite presence in the region of the Sainte-Baume for us to suggest that there must in all probability have been contact between them and the Provençal legend we are investigating.

To determine what form this might have taken, we must first try to unravel the history and development of the legend itself.

6

A Burgundian Detour

'Don't you find it amusing?' Philippe once asked me, with a grin. 'This return to an almost medieval acceptance of Authority!'

What he had in mind was the way in which those who reject the Provençal legend on principle – an unscientific approach, surely – seem only too willing to accept unquestioningly the theories of anyone who tries to undermine it. In our day, this largely means the writings of Victor Saxer.

Although Philippe may have been exaggerating to make his point, it is indeed true that Saxer's conclusions are repeated and propagated as if they were gospel truth – all too often, one suspects, by those unaware of the less than convincing methods by which he sometimes arrived at them. There have been earlier critics, of course, including Lefèbre d'Étaples in the sixteenth century, Jean de Launoy in the seventeenth and, more recently, Duchesne who flourished at the turn of the twentieth. Duchesne's massive three-volume work entitled *Fastes épiscopaux de l'ancienne Gaule* sounds and looks impressive. Yet in it he devotes a mere handful of pages to the Provençal legend – a reprint, in fact, of an article that had appeared in the *Annales du midi*. By contrast, Saxer dedicated a large part of his career to demolishing the Provençal tradition.

The basic premise of all these critics, other than the belief that the tradition cannot possibly be true, is that no early documents exist to support it. Duchesne speaks of a 'silence de mille ans'. This supposed thousand-year silence would not in itself be surprising. For at least 200 years, from the eighth to the tenth century, Provence was subjected to an unremitting series of devastating invasions, most notably from Saracens and the even more destructive Charles Martel ('The Hammer'). Monasteries, churches, indeed entire towns were besieged, pillaged, burned and destroyed. From AD 465 to 969 Arles, for example, was besieged ten times, sacked and pillaged seven times. Throughout Provence, the loss of documents, manuscripts and archives – secular as well as ecclesiastical – was considerable. Any dealing with the Mary Magdalen of Provençal tradition will have been no exception. Nevertheless, the legend is dismissed as having been invented in the Burgundian monastery of Vézelay in the middle of the eleventh century.

It is undeniable that Vézelay with its magnificent twelfth-century church dedicated to La Madeleine – the largest Romanesque church in the world – does figure prominently in the history of the legend. The original foundation, by Girart de Roussillon, dates from around 860. This was a convent at the foot of the hill, in the hamlet now called Saint-Pierre. In 873 Viking raiders sacked and pillaged the area, and the buildings were rapidly abandoned. Girart himself died around 877, but a new monastic settlement – of men this time – began to form on top of the hill. For a century or so, little is heard of the place.

By the eleventh century, a period of ignorance and laxity had set in, to such an extent that the monastery had become an object of scandal for the locals of the town that had grown up around it. In addition, from 1030–33 the region experienced one of the worst famines ever. Disorder, violence, and pillage were rampant, as people tried not to die of starvation. Even cannibalism was reported. This unsettled state of affairs lasted beyond the duration of the famine itself, so much so that the Church was called upon to exert its influence. At the various councils that were convened for this purpose, the relics of certain saints were produced and honoured. Various miracles were reported to have occurred, greatly impressing the general public.

Even so, peace did not prevail. It is said, for example, that a certain knight, who had been unjustly imprisoned in these lawless times, was so tightly clamped in irons and in such a cruel fashion, that he could not move at all. In desperation he began to pray to Mary Magdalen for help. After a time, his chains did miraculously break. Having gained his freedom, he carried these same chains all the way to Vézelay, where he deposited them in thanksgiving. People had started to believe that Mary was associated with the monastery. Exactly why is not clear.

In 1037 an attempt was made to rectify the laxness of the monks, with Geoffroy de Cluny, a pious man, now in charge. It seems to have been at this time that Mary Magdalen began to be venerated at the monastery. Certainly there had never been any previous tradition, nor had she until then been a patron of the abbey or its church. Since Geoffroy was intent on reform, it is possible that it was in this context that he began to promote Mary Magdalen, model par excellence of reform. A document from Pope Leo IX dated 1050 – a reply to an earlier letter – says nothing about any relics but, in the preamble, does assume that Mary Magdalen is (or, rather, has become) one of the monastery's patron saints.

> Leo, Bishop, servant of the servants of God, to Geoffroy, abbot of Vézelay, a monastery founded in honour of Our Lord Jesus Christ, venerating his holy Mother, the Apostles Peter and Paul, and Saint Mary Magdalen, and also to Geoffroy's successors . . .

This is the oldest written record of any connection between her and Vézelay. At this date, she has not yet become its chief patron, clearly coming last in the list of names.

Nevertheless, people came gradually to believe, as did the monks themselves, that they possessed her body. As a result, the monastery began to become a place of pilgrimage. When people started to ask how the body, which was never displayed, came to be in Vézelay, the embarrassed monks were at a loss. It seems that it was in order to provide an answer that a narrative was composed. The hesitation and uncertainty with which it was put together can be seen in the two very different versions that were produced.

In the first, Eudes (the first abbot) and the knight Adalème go to Arles with a detachment of soldiers. They bring back, not one but two bodies – that of Maximin as well. In the second version, it is the monk Badilon who goes to Provence, sent by Eudes and Girart de Roussillon. All talk of Maximin's body now disappears. The dates are given variously as 749, 771 and 882. As can be seen, two of the years cited predate the very existence of the monastery.

In neither version is the precise location of the tomb ever adequately described. Beyond mentioning the initial enquiry at Arles, the first version is entirely vague. In the second, the misleading reference to Arles is dropped in favour of Aix. Yet the wording is such that confusion began to arise, suggesting that the intended reference was to the *town* of Aix rather than its *comté*. The location of the tombs remains vague. Later reproducers of Vézelay's version of events compounded the confusion, as did artists, spreading the belief that the tombs were in Aix itself. Typical of this vagueness and confusion is the account given in *The Golden Legend* in the thirteenth century, probably the most familiar text of all: 'And when the monk [Badilon] came to the said city [Aix], he found it all destroyed of paynims. Then by adventure he found the sepulchre [...].'

François Rochefort's *Vie de la belle et chère Madeleine,* written for Louise de Savoie at the beginning of the sixteenth century, provides an example of how the confusion between town and territory persisted. Mary was buried in a beautiful sepulchre in Aix, he writes, centuries after her sarcophagus had been rediscovered and visited by hundreds of thousands of pilgrims in Saint-Maximin. Among them, in 1516, had been Louise de Savoie herself, along with her son François I and his queen. Like others before and since, Rochefort seems to have obtained his information from authors ignorant of Provence and who, like himself, had never visited the places in question.

Returning to the matter of the legend's origin, the critics are indeed correct to claim that it dates from the eleventh century. That is, the Vézelay versions. In these, Mary's body is said to have been rescued from a Provence laid waste by marauding Saracens in the eighth or ninth century, depending on the version consulted. At that time Provence was, admittedly, attached to Burgundy, forming a single kingdom. Nevertheless, one wonders why Vézelay waited some 200 years before ever making its claim to possess her relics. So far as I am aware, no one has addressed this question.

Vézelay's fame and the story of how it had acquired such an illustrious saint began to spread, especially after 1103 when Pope Pascal II lifted the ban which had been imposed on the pilgrimage by the Bishops of Autun (in whose diocese Vézelay was situated). Such papal bulls as this – and indeed the earlier one of 1050 – should not be seen as evidence of exceptional intervention; for, since its inception, the monastery had been subject directly to the papacy. Yet, though not an official notification of authenticity, Pascal's document did refer to 'Mary Magdalen's tomb'. Vézelay was all set to reach the high point of its glory.

The abbey's central location in western Europe was also in its favour. It was an excellent place of rendezvous, an ideal staging post, whether for pilgrimages to Compostella, crusades to the Holy Land, or simply meetings of kings, princes and rulers. It was here in 1166, for example, that Thomas à Becket, exiled Archbishop of Canterbury, pronounced his solemn condemnation of Henry II.

Provence, still laid waste after centuries of invasion and destruction, was hardly in a position to counter the claims of the Burgundian monks. Yet Vézelay's stock was to fall as quickly as it had risen.

The doubts had never entirely subsided, even after the promulgation of the legend designed to account for them. Moreover, the relics had still never been displayed, nor had the tomb. The numbers of pilgrims fell as suspicions increased. In an attempt to revive the monastery's fame, it was eventually decided that the supposed tomb would be located and opened.

The details of the event, which took place on 11 September 1265, are vague and unconvincing. A search was made under the main altar where a long bronze container was discovered. It contained 'certain relics' wrapped in two pieces of silk, along with a quantity of female hair. An equally vague, extremely brief and undated text of authentication by a King Charles was also said to have been discovered alongside the relics.

The exact identity of this Charles is not spelled out. The name was presumably chosen to suggest a period that would tally with the lifetime of the abbey's founder, Girart, and that of its first abbot, Eudes, both of whom are mentioned in the narrative. Yet whether we opt for Charles the son of Lothair I, Charles the Bald, Charles the Fat or even Charles the Simple, serious problems of chronology arise. Finally, why was the authenticating document not drawn up by a bishop or similar church dignitary, as was customary according to Church canons?

The reason given in the legend for transferring the body to Vézelay was in order to remove it from an area subject to invasion and pillage. Yet the same legend describes Aix as already having been laid waste, the marauders presumably having moved on. Moreover, Vézelay seems hardly to have been a more secure spot, for the Vikings continued to ravage Burgundy until well into the late tenth century.

In short, nothing about the two Vézelay versions hangs together.

Contemporary visitors seem to have thought likewise, for further efforts to convince had to be made. It was decided that the relics would after all be solemnly displayed. Knowing of his great interest in Mary Magdalen, the monks invited the future St Louis, whose pious reputation would give added weight to the ceremony. He determined a date and came with his three sons. Yet the occasion – which took place some two years later, on Sunday 24 April 1267 – seems to have been a disappointment. Far from reinvigorating the pilgrimage, it marked the beginning of its end.

❦

Despite the Burgundian claim to have possessed Mary's relics since the ninth century, the entries in the grotto's *Journalier* show that pilgrims had never stopped coming to the Sainte-Baume and Saint-Maximin. Indeed, no trace can be found in any Provençal source to suggest that the body ever left the area. Even at the time of Vézelay's apogee, its own tradition seems to have remained intact. This is reflected in the letter circulated in 1070 by *Rostan de Fos* (Archbishop of Aix, 1056–82), in which he requests alms for the construction of a new church, to remedy the ravages caused by the Saracens. He reminds the faithful, as if it were a well-known tradition among them, how Mary Magdalen and Maximin came to Marseilles and then to Aix, where they founded the first church, dedicating it to the Saviour and his Resurrection, with Maximin as its first bishop. Whose tombs, he adds, are 'chez nous' (*apud nos*). By this the Archbishop does not mean that they are to be found in Aix but 'here in Provence'; more specifically, 'here in our diocese', as Saint-Maximin was until the Revolution.

Then there is the 1102 Bull of Pascal II – the same, ironically, who corresponded with Vézelay, agreeing that the ban on their pilgrimage should be lifted – in which he authorizes Pierre III of Aix to wear a *pallium* for the feast days of Mary Magdalen and Maximin. In 1103, according to the Charter of Consecration of the new Basilica of Saint-Sauveur, the consecrating bishops reminded the congregation of the founders of the first oratory in Aix, Mary Magdalen and Maximin.

Fra Salimbene's description of his visit to the Sainte-Baume in 1224 is one I have already quoted from. Indeed, by the twelfth and thirteenth centuries chronicles, hagiographies and liturgical texts all stated that Mary's body had been removed to Vézelay from its initial burial place which, so it was stressed, had been situated in Provence. It was common knowledge. Vézelay's own legend had seen to that! 'It has for a long time been known for certain, far and wide,' it reads, 'that the body of Saint Mary Magdalen was buried in the territory (*in territorio*) of Aix by the holy Bishop Maximin, whose remains were also laid to rest there.'

For a long time ... How long?

Do any accounts exist of Mary's arrival and activities in Provence *prior* to those promoted by Vézelay?

❧

The Life of Saint Mary Magdalen and of her Sister Martha would seem to be one such account. Seven manuscript copies have so far been found. Faillon, who did the lion's share of research into this matter in the nineteenth century – publishing his findings in his two-volumed 'monumental' *Monuments inédits sur l'apostolat de Sainte Marie-Madeleine en Provence (1848)* – discovered that the copy held at Magdalen College, Oxford, carried a marginal attribution to Raban Maur. (Modern critics tend to mock Faillon's work, delighting to pick holes in details, which is not difficult to do. They seem far less inclined to admit their indebtedness to him.)

Rabanus Maurus (d.856), Archbishop of Mainz and one of the greatest scholars of the Carolingian age, was a friend of Alcuin, under whom he had studied at Tours. Several early hymns have been attributed to him, most notably *Veni Creator Spiritus*. Yet was he the author of the *Life* that interests us? Only the Magdalen College copy explicitly says so, and it is dated *c.* 1409. The earliest of the seven manuscripts found so far, at Montpellier, is from the twelfth century and originated at the abbey of Clairvaux, situated not far from Vézelay. Yet it is easy to overlook the fact that all of these are 'copies'. By definition, the text from which the Montpellier manuscript was made must be older still. Nor was it necessarily the original.

Saxer claimed that the Montpellier manuscript was actually composed at Clairvaux, not simply copied there, in the twelfth century. As evidence, he claims that the text here and there reveals the influence of the spirituality of St Bernard, the monastery's great abbot. However, his examples are few in number and less than convincing. Moreover, they are all taken from the chapters which weave together events found in the Gospels. None are from the Provençal episode proper.

Moreover, in the fifty chapters which make up the *Life*, there is not a single mention of the transfer of Mary Magdalen's relics to Vézelay nor of her cult there. For a text supposedly composed in the second half of the twelfth century under the marked influence of St Bernard, such an omission is difficult to explain. All the more so since it was at Vézelay on Easter Sunday, 31 March 1146, that Bernard famously and rousingly preached the Second Crusade to an enthusiastic crowd so large that the building, despite its vast proportions, could not contain it.

There is no reason not to believe that this *Life* was composed long before Mary's documented association with Vézelay ever began, that is, before 1050. Faillon argued that it was indeed the work of Raban Maur. Yet many of those who disagree, such as the Bollandists Van Hecke and Bossüe, still date it to the ninth century.

Further evidence that this dating seems correct can be seen by consulting the *Old English Martyrology* of *c.* 850. The entry for 22 July (Mary's feast day) understandably reads like a one-page précis, a fact which in itself presupposes the existence of a longer text or at least a more fully developed oral tradition. Yet in it we find all the ingredients of Raban's *Life*: the identification with the unnamed sinner, the thirty years in isolation without food or drink, the angelic elevation, the cave, her discovery by a priest. Although the location of the cave is not spelled out – beyond saying that it was 'in the desert' – it is interesting to note that the saint commemorated on the previous day in this Martyrology is none other than Victor of Marseilles, eponym of Cassian's monastery.

Pseudo-Raban's is the longest known *Life*, consisting of fifty short chapters. The first thirty-four together form a narrative, based on the New Testament, dealing with events in Palestine up to Pentecost. Chapters 35 and 36 describe the dispersion of Jesus' followers throughout the Mediterranean basin, including Gaul. It is Chapters 37 to 50 which relate the evangelization of Provence by Maximin and Mary Magdalen from their base at Aix.

The author is highly critical of what he bluntly dismisses, in Chapter 39, as 'apocryphal' additions. The elevation by angels and the eating of nothing but 'celestial food' may well, he admits, have a mystical meaning. 'But as for her withdrawing into the Arabian desert [...] and that she remained there without clothing in a cave, seeing no man; that, being visited by some priest or other, she asked him for a garment – these and other such details are utterly false, borrowed by fabricators of fables from the story of the penitent Egyptian woman.'

His indignation seems to have got the better of him in this passage. For nowhere in Mary of Egypt's tale is it said that the desert into which she withdrew was that of Arabia. Rather, leaving Jerusalem, she crossed the River Jordan. Nor is there any reference to surviving only on 'celestial food' or being raised into the air by angels on a regular basis.

More interesting is the reference to living in a cave. No trace of this either can be found in the story of Mary of Egypt. Yet so important did this feature become in the Provençal tradition that we must later return to the question of its origin. If it is not derived from the story of Mary of Egypt, then from where?

The importance of the *Life* by pseudo-Raban is not its length, but the fact that it provides one more link in the chain of tradition. It establishes, first of all, that by the ninth century throughout Europe the belief that Mary Magdalen and Maximin had evangelized the area around Aix was well established; that elements from the story of Mary of Egypt had already been added to the legend; that

Mary had retired to a cave; and that her tomb and Maximin's were located at the town that was to be named after him.

More important still is the Prologue, which refers to yet older traditions, oral and written. After explaining that he will first assemble all the relevant Gospel material, the author states that he will then relate what happened to the followers of Jesus after his Ascension, according both to the tradition handed down by the Fathers and also to what they have left in their writings (*nobis patres nostri tradiderunt et in suis etiam reliquerunt scriptis*). He also makes clear that, in writing this *Life*, he will have recourse to 'ancient histories' or 'stories' (*veteres ... historiae*).

All in all, this takes us further back still than the ninth century, to a time when the monastery at Vézelay had not even been founded. Vézelay – to borrow a phrase traditionally used in French guide-books – *vaut le détour*. It is a phrase which can, of course, be understood in quite the opposite sense to the one intended!

7

Veteres Historiae

We have seen that pseudo-Raban, writing in the ninth century, was dismissive of what he termed the fables and apocryphal additions to Mary Magdalen's story. It follows that he must have known of a purer tradition, one with which he was able to compare the more fanciful versions. It is these *veteres historiae*, these 'ancient histories' – as he calls them, using the plural – that he admits to having drawn on in composing his own account.

Does any trace of them survive? Faillon believed he had found one such early text, which he named the *Ancienne Vie*. I reproduce it below in my own translation.

> Although most people have to hand the longer story which tells how, in accordance with divine goodness, St Mary Magdalen sailed with St Maximin and arrived in the region of Aix, in the Kingdom of Provence – as is related in the Life of this holy bishop – we have nevertheless made a point of publishing this little summary so that those not yet acquainted with the above longer Life, might at least know the truth of what it contains.

❧

> After the glorious Resurrection of the Lord, His triumphant Ascension and the sending of the Holy Spirit, the Paraclete (Who filled the hearts of the Disciples when they were still trembling through fear of temporal ills and Who gave them knowledge of divers languages), the believers were all assembled together with the holy women, among whom was Mary

the Mother of Jesus, as is related by Luke the Evangelist.

The word of God spread and the number of faithful increased daily to the extent that, as a result of the preaching of the Apostles, several thousand people sold their property; for all shared everything in common, being of one mind and one heart.

The Jewish priests, together with the Scribes and the Pharisees, inflamed with jealousy, stirred up persecution against the Church and, after putting to death Stephen the first martyr, drove far from Judaea almost all the other witnesses of Jesus Christ. Whilst this persecution was raging, the faithful that it had scattered travelled to various parts of the world, according as the Lord had assigned them, to preach the word of salvation to the Gentiles. With the Apostles at that time was St Maximin, one of the 72, a person commendable on account of the total integrity of his morals and famed for his teaching and his gift of working miracles. St Mary Magdalen, who lived in his company – just as the Blessed Mary Ever-Virgin in that of St John the Evangelist, to whom the Lord had entrusted her – devoted herself to the care of this holy disciple.

During this diaspora, Maximin and Mary Magdalen went to the seashore. There they boarded a vessel and, after a favourable journey, arrived at Marseilles. Disembarking there, inspired by the Lord, they went into the Comté of Aix, distributing abundantly to all the seed of the divine word and endeavouring night and day, by their preaching, their fasts and their prayers, to attract to the knowledge and worship of Almighty God the people of this region, who were as yet unbelievers and not yet regenerated by the waters of baptism.

The Confessor and Pontiff Maximin governed the church at Aix for many years, attending faithfully to preaching, exorcising demons, raising dead people, giving sight to the blind, curing the lame and healing every sort of infirmity.

Now when the time drew near for Mary Magdalen to be delivered from the prison of her body, she saw that Jesus Christ – to whose service she had dedicated herself so completely – was calling her in His mercy to the glory of the heavenly Kingdom, in order to give for ever the food of heaven to her who had faithfully supported Him in temporal life, when He had appeared in human form. She died the eleventh day before the Kalends of August [= 22 July], the angels rejoicing as she joined the company of the heavenly Virtues, for she had been found worthy to enjoy the splendour of [divine] glory and to see the King of the Ages in all His beauty.

Taking her holy body, Bishop Maximin embalmed it with various aromatic spices and placed it in a worthy mausoleum. Over her holy body he built a basilica of remarkable architecture. There one can see her tomb, which is of white marble. On it is sculpted how she sought out the Lord in the house of Simon and how, weeping and ashamed, in the midst of guests she rendered unto Him a courteous favour with perfumed oil.

Finally, the blessed Bishop Maximin, seeing approach the time at which the Holy Spirit had revealed to him that he would be taken from this life to receive from the goodness of the sovereign Judge the rewards of his labours, instructed that his burial be in the basilica we have mentioned and that his sarcophagus be placed next to the body of Mary Magdalen.

And so, after his holy death, he was honourably buried there by the faithful. Both saints make this place famous by the noteworthy miracles worked by their intercession in favour of those who call on them for the healing of soul or body.

With the passage of time, this church has become so holy that no king, prince or other person – however distinguished or esteemed in the eyes of the world – dare enter, without first having laid down his arms, without having divested himself of all feelings of brutal ferocity and, finally, without first having shown signs of a humble devotion. Never has any woman – of whatever position or rank or however reverent – dared enter this holy temple. This monastery is called the Abbey of Saint-Maximin. It is situated in the Comté of Aix and is richly endowed with possessions and ornaments. It was on the sixth day before the Ides of June that St Maximin died and was joyfully crowned by the Lord. To Whom be honour and glory for ever and ever. Amen.

Faillon found three copies of this *Ancienne Vie*, in tenth-century manuscripts but which were copies of older ones still. As he points out, this version certainly seems to be even more ancient than the interpolated texts pseudo-

Raban had before him in the ninth century. There is no enforced boarding of a ship at the hands of persecutors, no mention of it being bereft of sail or rudder. There is no cave, no angelic elevation; no celestial food; no visit in the desert by a priest; nor any of the other additions from Mary of Egypt's history. Mary Magdalen's date of death is given as 22 July (her traditional feast day) not Good Friday (as for Mary of Egypt).

The Franciscan Damien Voreux – who reproduced the text in his 1963 book *Sainte Marie-Madeleine, quelle est donc cette femme?* – comments that it has the precision and concision of a martyrology. Interestingly, the Prologue refers to a *Life* of St Maximin. It is thus probable that this *Ancienne Vie* – rather than itself being an independent *Life* of Mary Magdalen – is in fact an extract from that, now lost, of Maximin.

Faillon dates the text to the sixth or fifth century for the following reasons.

Firstly, from the seventh century onwards the hagiographic style becomes characterized by a false eloquence, by standardized eulogies, a proliferation of adjectives, and an excessive stress on the miraculous. Earlier texts are – as is this – simpler, more sober, with fewer miracles and fewer quotations from the Gospels.

He next points to certain terminologies. Maximin is never, for example, styled *archipraesul*, 'Archbishop' (this being a later title, used by pseudo-Raban, for example) but as *pontifex*, *antistes* or *confessor*. These are more in keeping with fifth- and sixth-century usage. As for the part of France pinpointed, it is styled *Aquensis Comitatus* – the *Comté d'Aix*. At this period, as Gregory of Tours and others testify, each town had its *comte*, the territory over which his jurisdiction extended being called a *comté*. This contrasts with the term *territorium*, used in the much later Vézelay version.

The comment about wearing armour in church is connected with the use of the word 'Kingdom' [*regnum*]. The reference is not to the ninth-century Carolingian period, Faillon argues, but to the fifth- and sixth-century rule of the Goths, Visigoths and Ostrogoths, several of whom had their seat at Arles, as is clear from the *Life* of St Caesarius, the early sixth-century bishop of the town. Provence was indeed called a Kingdom at this time. It seems that these Goths – noted, of course, for the 'brutal ferocity' mentioned in the text – really did enter holy places still sporting their shields and lances. The author here takes care to point out this notable exception.

The ban on women visitors is explained simply by the fact that the tombs were in a monastery church.

If Faillon's dating is correct, we can conclude that as early as the fifth or sixth century it was widely believed that Maximin, one of the seventy-two, had been the first bishop of Aix, a town he had evangelized with Mary Magdalen; that both were buried at the place which later became known as Saint-Maximin. (Perhaps an abbreviation of *L'Abbaye de Saint-Maximin.*) Their tombs were already a place of special devotion, even attracting kings and princes.

The church housing the tombs was already so ancient that people were willing to accept the traditional view that St Maximin himself had built it. We know that churches did exist even before 313, the date from which Constantine gave Christianity legal status. This is clear from the reference to the one erected in honour of the martyrs of Lyons, shortly after their deaths in 177, as mentioned by Gregory of Tours in his *Glory of the Martyrs* (§ 48).

However, it was evidently *not* believed that Mary had withdrawn to a cave. Yet, far from posing a problem, this leads us to the heart of the original tradition.

Faillon also found three manuscripts of a *Life* of Mary Magdalen which already contained several additions and which he judged to be from the seventh century. His dating seems reasonable, since this version must be later than the uncontaminated fifth- to sixth-century *Ancienne Vie*, yet earlier than pseudo-Raban's own ninth-century text, which criticizes these same additions. In fact, this particular version reproduces verbatim the *Ancienne Vie* but (as well as adding a pious, hortatory conclusion) interpolates a lengthy section immediately after the mention of Maximin having ruled the church at Aix for many years.

The insertion is almost three times longer than the original text. In it appears, perhaps for the first time in written form, the eye-catching details of Mary's withdrawal to a 'desert' – a word which then could simply have signified a 'deserted place', its exclusive association with sand being relatively modern. Also added is her elevation into the angelic spheres seven times a day, at the hours of canonical prayer, and her ability to abstain from normal food. Here, too, we find the cave making its grand appearance.

From the very criticisms of pseudo-Raban, it is clear that the version he knew was a later one still. For in the text under discussion there is no reference to the details which he found most objectionable. For example, that the place to where Mary had fled was 'the deserts of Arabia'; that she was 'naked' and had asked the priest who discovered her for an item of clothing before she would stay and talk to him. Nor is there any appeal, regarding the veracity of all this, to the authority of the first-century Jewish historian Josephus or the second-century Church historian Hegesippus.

Examining more closely the seventh-century interpolated version reproduced by Faillon, we find several interesting details.

To begin with, a location which, though not specifically named – is fairly accurately identifiable:

> In the *comté* of Aix [...] a harsh deserted place [...] a cavern in the side of a very steep mountain [...] A certain priest [...] a religious [...] who was in charge of a small congregation 100 stadia from the place where, unknown to all, Saint Mary Magdalen led the life of a solitary. Each year, from the first Sunday in Lent, it was his habit to withdraw further into the wilderness in order to perfect himself by hymns, prayers and bodily abstinences. Therefore, although unaware of the miracle that the Lord had wrought here in connection with his saintly beloved, he had built himself a cell 12 stadia away, near a small spring.

To anyone familiar with the Sainte-Baume region these topographical details sound familiar and make good sense, especially the precise distances quoted. 100 stadia equals 18.5 kilometres, exactly the distance from the cave to Saint-Maximin. 12 stadia equals 2.5 kilometres, the distance from the cave to the spring and hermitage. Of course, the place could not be designated as the 'Sainte-Baume', since at this early period it had no such name. (The name seems to have become official around the time of King René in the fifteenth century.)

To return to the interpolated text, the priest-monk who discovers Mary is entrusted with informing Bishop Maximin of their meeting and their conversation. 'Tell him that on the most holy day of the Resurrection of my Lord Jesus Christ, which is approaching, he should go and celebrate Lauds in the oratory that he himself built. Let him go alone. There, praising my Saviour and having being transported by angels, he will find me waiting.' This is done. The text then continues as follows. 'Drawing near, as we have found it expressed *in the books of the same Blessed Maximin*, he saw that Mary's face was shining in such a manner that it would have been easier to look at the rays of the sun.' Before assuming that this is merely figurative writing, we do well to recall the experience of the nineteenth-century businessman Motovilov, when in the company of St Seraphim.

Later in the service, Mary receives communion and shortly afterwards dies.

We can only wonder in frustration as to which 'books' the writer is here referring. Can we be any more successful in identifying the priest-monk of the narrative?

The author – who, as seen, seems to have known the area personally – was quite possibly one of the Cassianite monks who, from the fifth century, settled there. (The use of the terms *abbatia* and *monasterium* in the *Vie Ancienne* – and which are repeated here – clearly points to the presence of monks, as do the words *religious* and *congregation*.)

Who else can he be alluding to but John Cassian himself?

As he would be well aware, such a meeting would be totally anachronistic, which is probably why he refrains from actually naming John. Yet the signs are there: he is in charge of a community of monks; he follows the early Palestinian and Egyptian monastic custom of withdrawing into an isolated cell for the duration of Lent, in imitation of Jesus' own forty days in the desert. Indeed, it was in all likelihood none other than Cassian who imported this custom into southern France, where it is known to have been followed – as in the documented case of St Marius (d.555), whose *Life* by Dynamius has already been mentioned – before the Rule of St Benedict became widespread. Because of the fame of his coenobitic monastery of Saint-Victor at Marseilles, together with his insistence that the hermit's life was spiritually dangerous for those monks who had not already reached a level of maturity, Cassian's appreciation and personal experience of the value of solitude have tended to be overlooked. Yet in Part Three of the *Conferences* (19.5), he writes of how in Egypt he 'frequented with insatiable desire and all [his] heart the peaceful retreats of the desert and that life which can only be compared to the bliss of angels'. Moreover, in the Preface to this last group of Conferences he makes clear his aim of offering advice and instruction not simply to those monks who seek the common life, but to those who 'try to carry out the rule of the anchorites [...] which is almost unknown in this country'. In his book devoted to Cassian, Chadwick rightly comments that the Cassianite monk 'was aware, more aware than later monks of the West would be, that outside his cloister lay the woods and islands, where some were called to a higher and contemplative vocation, the silent and unceasing prayer of the anchorite in his solitude'.

Even the detail of Mary's being elevated seven times a day at the hours of canonical prayers could owe something to Cassian. At least, he devoted two entire books of his *Institutions* (Bks 2 and 3) to the topic since, as he says, the soldier of Christ 'should [...] learn the system of the canonical prayers and psalms which was long ago arranged by the holy Fathers in the East' (Bk 2.1). He seeks not simply to impart information but to establish more uniformity of practice, and to give an understanding of the rationale and history of the practice, pointing out that it was in his own time at his own original monastery (in Bethlehem) that the practice of chanting the seventh of these Hours (Prime) was introduced.

It is surely significant, too, that the place where the spring and the signs of a hermitage are still to be found, on the plateau below the Pic or Baou St-Cassien, is itself named the Grand St-Cassien. Those who have consulted the cadastres and other public documents have never found that any other names were used for these places.

Today there is nothing at the Grand St-Cassien but ruins. Yet the stones, the tiles, and the bases of columns all seem to point to its having been a small monastery or oratory, perhaps built around the very hermitage mentioned in the seventh-century text. Certainly, locals questioned in the nineteenth century invariably replied that this is what everyone had always believed. Towards the end of the fifteenth century, two German pilgrims visited the spot. One of them, Hans von Waltheym, notes in his diary (1474) that the roof had fallen in, the beams lying about on the ground. He writes:

> This cell is very isolated and wild, hidden in the forest in a lonely place, far from people. And the good holy priest [the *gardien* of the grotto] told us he hoped, God willing, to reconstruct the cell so as to spend the final years of his life there.

Further evidence for an early dating of this version – interpolated though it is – is the fact that there is none of the excessively penitential tone that we find in later centuries. Instead, Mary Magdalen is depicted as wishing 'to devote herself to a more intense form of contemplation' in order to 'develop more fully the better part that she had chosen', this being an echo of Jesus' defence of her before Martha in Luke 10. It is surely in connection with this that the day of her death is now given as Easter Sunday – not 22 July as in the *Ancienne Vie*, nor Good Friday like Mary of Egypt – in what is a clear reference to that first privileged Resurrection appearance to Mary in the garden. In this symbolic, if anachronistic, meeting between her and the fifth-century inspirer of western monasticism, she is presented not just as the Apostle of the Resurrection but as the patron saint of all who would lead the contemplative life.

Nevertheless, it cannot have been true that Mary spent years in ascetic isolation in the Sainte-Baume region. Conditions there in the first century were very different from what they later became. In the first place, it was not especially isolated. A stream of pagan pilgrims still made the journey from Marseilles, where the temple of Artemis (Diana) was still frequented, to her sacred forest and cave.

There is a strong tradition that, shortly after landing in Marseilles, Mary – rather like Paul when he arrived in Athens – sought out the most logical spot to preach the good news to the pagans: the square in front of the above temple. It is conceivable that she would sooner or later have followed these same pagans up to the cave, perhaps on the occasion of a special feast. There she would have again had an excellent opportunity to spread the word to the assembled pilgrims.

However, in 391, when Theodosius the First issued the edict whereby Christianity became the official religion of the Empire, he simultaneously outlawed pagan cults and closed all pagan sites. Interestingly, it was Cassian's mentor, Patriarch of Constantinople John Chrysostom, who in 401 is said to have led the mob which destroyed Diana's temple in Ephesus. Some of its columns were reused in the construction of the Hagia Sofia basilica in Constantinople. In 401 Cassian was himself still one of Chrysostom's deacons. Had he perhaps been present in Ephesus? Even if not, he would surely have known about it. It was only a few years later (*c.* 408–10) that he arrived in Marseilles, where Diana's sister-temple would also have been closed by Theodosius' edict. Its associated cave at the

Sainte-Baume would gradually have been abandoned by pagan pilgrims. Was it Cassian, the Ephesian affair fresh in his mind, who had the idea of adapting it to a Christian purpose?

What is certain is that before his arrival there is no tradition of Mary Magdalen at the cave and no trace of additions to her story from that of Mary of Egypt. As seen, the earliest known interpolated text dates from the seventh century. Thus it is probable that these borrowings began to be made some time between the fifth century and the seventh. The Cassianites would seem to be the most likely people responsible, for this was the very period during which they were spreading out from Marseilles into the surrounding countryside. (As mentioned, it is clear from the *Life* of St Marius by Dynamius that Mary of Egypt was known about in Provence at least as early as 601.) Moreover, in 'establishing' Mary Magdalen in the cave, they would simply have been doing what was being done at this period in countless places across Europe: 'baptizing' a pagan holy site.

There is admittedly no mention of either Mary Magdalen or Mary of Egypt in Cassian's books, which were written at the request of other people for a very specific purpose. (He does, however, in the *Conferences* identify Mary the sister of Martha as being Luke's unnamed sinner, in a context where the stress is on contemplation.) Yet it is worth repeating that he was fluent in Greek and so could well have known of the Egyptian penitent's tale long before it was translated into Latin. (Many other people in the area spoke Greek, too. Even in the middle of the sixth century Caesarius, Bishop of Arles, was having to compose hymns in Greek, for the benefit of those of his flock who spoke nothing else.) Since Cassian himself had spent many years in Egypt and Palestine, as we saw, it is possible that he had heard of her story while it was still circulating in oral form (as the Preface to the first written account said it had) and had passed it on to his monks.

Even if these suggested origins and developments are

mistaken, what is evident is that any interpolation from the life of Mary of Egypt into the story of Mary Magdalen suggests that the latter must already have existed, and in written form.

❧

Nevertheless, say the critics, all early dates for the Sainte-Baume legend must be automatically dismissed, since no document prior to the twelfth century locates the cave. (Even in these, it is described not by its present name – a name which, as mentioned earlier, did not become fixed until the fifteenth century – but as being '14 or 15 miles east of Marseilles'.) This may indeed be true, for it is only in about 1000 – after the centuries of invasion, occupation and destruction – that Saint-Victor is able to begin sorting out its property and possessions. By the first quarter of the tenth century, Marseilles had reached the lowest point in a long period of decline. Its maritime trade had been reduced to nothing, its land abandoned by farmers who no longer felt safe, life having long become a matter of fear of Saracen invasion whether by land or sea. The town's bishop (Drogon) had left with many citizens to seek refuge in the ancient citadel now called Saint-Blaise, just north of Martigues. All in all, Marseilles had become less extensive than the ancient Greek settlement ever had been.

In the second half of the tenth century the next bishop, Honoratus II, began to restore his diocese and to rebuild the abandoned monastery. After an experimental period, he opted for the Rule of St Benedict. Under Wilfred (first abbot) and then Ysarn, the monastery rose again from its ashes. Ysarn built an upper church on top of the ancient *martyrium* and the associated buildings, which then became the crypt. This new church was consecrated in 1040.

The documents drawn up as part of Saint-Victor's attempts to flourish again were not designed to establish a new state of affairs, but rather to sort out and return so far as possible to the situation that existed prior to the centuries of invasions and upheavals. Its ecclesiastical dependencies, lands and other possessions, or what remained of them, had long since passed into secular ownership. Thus any dates they bear may be misleadingly late. Furthermore, we are concerned to date, not merely a document, but a tradition. Though this is habitually overlooked by sceptics, these are not the same thing.

Another of Saxer's suggestions is that the story of Mary Magdalen at the Sainte-Baume was invented by the monastery at Montrieux, the same which Gherardo Petrarch entered. He makes this claim solely on the basis of a twelfth-century manuscript of the story, found in Berne, to which the copyist had added the information that the cave was 'not far from Montrieux'. Naturally, the Carthusian order, founded in 1084 and specializing in contemplative life in 'deserts', would be interested in the ascetic withdrawal of someone styled the 'greatest of contemplatives' – but only if that was what she had already become in the popular mind. If the tradition had not already existed, why would they have chosen Mary Magdalen for this role? On what basis would they have believed that she came to Provence? And why would they have chosen this particular cave, when there are many more in the area, several nearer to Montrieux? The Carthusians, a strictly enclosed order, would have had absolutely no interest in being *gardiens* of the cave or in greeting the many pilgrims that would be attracted by their invented story, or in providing for their religious needs. Moreover, Saxer's hypothesis conveniently ignores the list of visitors to the cave, which they already associated with Mary Magdalen, as recorded from the eighth century onwards in the *Journalier*. It also inexplicably overlooks the fact that Montreux itself was originally a Cassianite foundation, as the monastery's own website states. Its own archives, too, as we saw in our Prologue, contain the legend of the wealthy Italian pilgrim who, healed after prayers offered in the cave, founded Montrieux as a result. It would seem to be the cave that gave rise to the monastery, rather than vice versa. Of course, of all western monastic orders it is precisely the Carthusians who are Cassian's natural successors, and closest in spirit and practice to the desert spirtuality he introduced.

As for the founder of Saint-Victor, Saxer also claims that the driving force behind Provençal monasticism was not in any case Cassian (whose role in the Mary Magdalen tradition he thus discounts) but Honoratus of Lérins. This strangely overlooks Cassian's friendship with and influence on Honoratus, to whom he dedicated his second book of *Conferences*. Moreover, as Honoratus was well aware, it was Cassian who had first-hand experience of the Palestinian and Egyptian monasticism to which they both looked for their inspiration.

❧

During one of my conversations with him, I asked Philippe whether there were any Cassianite remains at the cave itself.

'Well, there was a fifth-century altar table. I believe it is now somewhere in the basilica in Saint-Maximin. But you know, when I first arrived,' he replied, 'I was rather surprised to be told, as a well-founded tradition, that the very first Cassianite monks had based themselves in the lower part of the grotto – the darkest and dampest part of all!'

I had myself seen it awash with water that had seeped in during a summer storm. As for its darkness, you would need a torch, were it not for the votive candles.

'One day,' he continued, 'I suddenly realized that at that time this part of the cave was completely open and capable of receiving the sun's rays at certain times of day. It was the building of the small monastery in the fourteenth century onto this part of the rock face which blocked up the large opening.'

Anyone who has visited the place will immediately see the validity of Philippe's point. An internal doorway giving straight onto the interior of the cave from the monastery is all that survives to remind us of the original configuration.

'But it just goes to show,' he added, 'that you should be careful before dismissing what seems to be far-fetched.'

❧

In attempting to trace the history of these *veteres historiae*, we must never forget that the tradition of Mary leading an ascetic life up at the cave, though much older than the twelfth-century hypothesis of the sceptics, is later than the original Provençal legend. This simply has her arriving in Provence by a regular shipping line, helping to evangelize Marseilles, then Aix and the surrounding area, before being buried at the place which became known, after the Bishop with whom she travelled here and worked, as Saint-Maximin. Nonetheless, it was probably inevitable that the cave – with its romantic appeal, its tantalisingly remote yet visible presence overlooking the sacred forest – would come to assume the larger role in the telling of the story down the centuries.

'What's *that* up there?' I recall being asked by a fascinated Frenchman, who had simply been touring the area. 'Can you walk to it? How long does it take?' I suspect it is a conversation that is regularly repeated outside the winter months.

In addition, the fact that Mary's story was largely spread by monasteries perhaps further explains the emphasis on the eremitic. Yet, even if her life in the Sainte-Baume area is largely or indeed entirely apocryphal, we must be grateful that – by its very romantic character – it also kept alive the original, more important belief that it was in this part of Provence that Mary fulfilled her apostolic mission and was laid to rest.

It is time to leave the Cave and to consider in more detail the Coffin.

Part Two

The Coffin

8

Saint-Maximin

'Saint-Maximin is a miserable hole between Aix and Draguignan.' So wrote Prosper Mérimée, author of *Carmen*, in his *Notes d'un voyage dans le Midi de la France* of 1835. In his capacity as Inspector General of Historical Monuments, Mérimée was concerned, in the period following the ravages of the Revolution, to classify buildings and sites of interest. Modern travel writers have been scarcely more flattering. Yet as you approach, two things contradict such negative write-ups.

Firstly, placards on the outskirts proudly inform you that you are approaching the 'Troisième Tombeau de la Chrétienneté'. The phrase is Lacordaire's, the tomb in question being, naturally, that of Mary Magdalen – third in importance after those of Christ and Peter.

Even more striking, however, particularly if you arrive from the Sainte-Baume or on the somewhat elevated *autoroute*, is the size of the basilica. As large as many a cathedral, it dwarfs the low-lying overgrown village, whose population even now amounts to less than 13,000. One can only wonder at the impression it must have made in the Middle Ages, as it rose to replace the earlier small church.

It is when Mérimée enters this building that the tone of his report noticeably changes, as my translation tries to show.

> The Basilica has a certain fame in Provence, where Gothic buildings are very rare. It is a fame well deserved, partly on

account of its size and the height of its three naves as well as the elegance of its apse.

The parish priest of Saint-Maximin is an educated cleric and a man of some wit. I was congratulating him on the attractive darkened colour of the stones inside his church, when he smiled and told me that he had taken considerable pains to preserve the noble patina with which Time has covered them. It seems that the town council in its wisdom had decided that the interior should be given a coat of whitewash. The parish priest had protested in vain, no one taking his opposition into account. When the day came for the work to be carried out, the painters with their brushes and ladders assembled at the door of the church, only to find it closed. They asked around for the keys; but the parish priest, in whose possession they were, proved not to be at home. They had to resign themselves to making a retreat. However, they were not beaten yet. Abandoning all hope of entering the building with the permission of the parish priest, they plotted to gain access the following Sunday during Mass and, once the service was over, to start work. Fortunately, the worthy cleric guessed what they were up to. Considering that it was better for his parishioners to do without a Mass than to see their church made a mess of, he never turned up at the altar. 'And,' he told me, 'I would have absented myself for a month, if necessary.' The inhabitants of Saint-Maximin – finding themselves, as it were, excommunicated – put the blame on the town council, which was obliged shamefacedly to lift the siege and to dismiss the painters once and for all. How desirable it would be, if France had many more parish priests like that of Saint-Maximin!

The choir is adorned with beautifully carved panelling dating from 1692. The pulpit and the sacristy have finely worked panelling, too. I complimented the parish priest on them and asked how he had managed to ensure that the beadles and cleaners took proper care of them. 'I brush and varnish them myself,' he replied. 'Do you think I would rely on ignoramuses to preserve these beautiful things?'

On leaving the church, I wrote to the *Ministre de l'Intérieur* to beg him to donate a painting to Saint-Maximin. There is no church in France more worthy of receiving *objets d'art*.

❧

Built onto the northern flank of the basilica is the no less interesting *Couvent Royal*, 'Couvent' being here used in the older sense. This was never a nunnery, but the monastery built by Charles II of Anjou for the Dominican monks who were installed in 1295, a few years after his rediscovery of the relics, replacing the Saint-Victor monks and what remained of the more modest buildings associated with them.

After many ups and downs, the Dominicans finally left the premises for Toulouse in 1957 and the place has now become an elegant hotel-restaurant. The cells have been transformed into attractive rooms, in most cases preserving something of the original feel. It is also a venue for cultural and musical events.

I became unexpectedly aware of this on my first stay there. This was in the west wing, now called the Lacordaire wing, after the energetic Dominican who caused it to be restored in 1859. Unpacking my case, I had taken out my copy of the little volume which he penned in 1860 to celebrate the climax of his life's work: *Sainte Marie-Madeleine*. Mine was only a third edition, but attractive nonetheless, with its black leather spine and black and yellow marbled boards. I looked again at the delicately written dedication: *A Madame Vautier, née Lecoq. Que Sainte Madeleine bénisse abondamment sa digne protégée et les chers siens.* Followed by an undecypherable signature. Not for the first time, I wondered who Madame Vautier was, and what had become of her.

'One cannot set foot on Provençal soil,' writes Lacordaire, 'without stumbling across the memory of Saint Mary Magdalen at every turn.'

I had placed the book on my table and thrown open the small Gothic-style window that gave onto the cloister below, with its garden of abundant and varied vegetation. To my surprise, I was greeted from a nearby window with the sound of an obviously professional tenor practising his scales. When I later went downstairs for an apéritif, I saw what must have been his name on the posters advertising that evening's concert and which had thus far escaped my notice.

In opening the window, I had wanted to get a view of the old well in the centre of the garden. Rumour has it that, two metres down, there is the beginning of a secret tunnel that leads up towards the Sainte-Baume. Whether or not this exists, it is certainly in this well that the relics of Mary Magdalen have been hidden during times of crisis, such as the pillage of the town by the forces of Charles V in 1536.

❧

The settlement that from the Middle Ages onwards became the little town of Saint-Maximin has always enjoyed a privileged geographical position. From as far back as can be traced, it has been a *lieu de passage*. The Nationale 7 and the modern motorway from Paris to Nice do no more than follow what was one of the most important Roman roads, linking Rome with Gaul and beyond. At Tourves, the road enters a wide, fertile plain that extends between the Mont Aurélien and the foothills of the Sainte-Victoire and the Sainte-Baume. Another old road branches off to the port of Marseilles, already ancient in the first century.

The name 'Saint-Maximin' – though mentioned in the fifth- or sixth-century *Ancienne Vie* – only became the standard way of referring to the settlement, rather than simply to the oratory, in the first decades of the eleventh century. This is clear from the documents and charters of the renascent monastery of Saint-Victor. Prior to that it was called by one of two names. Firstly, *Castrum Rodanas*, a citadel situated on high ground just outside the present town, and of which the present-day *quartier* known as *Collet-redon* is a reminder. Also used was the descriptive phrase *Villa Lata*, on account of the vast (*lata*) agricultural plain with its domain (*villa*), at the foot of the castrum. Here was located the ancient oratory erected by St Maximin and the small adjacent monastery, originally built by the first Cassianites when sent out from Marseilles to guard the tombs contained in the oratory. Admittedly, people may occasionally have used the name of the oratory to refer to the place itself. Nonetheless, there was no town or village as such.

The town as we know it today owes its existence to Charles II of Anjou, King of Naples, Count of Provence and nephew of St Louis. Before inheriting these titles and while still Prince of Salerno, he decided to erect a sumptuous basilica in honour of Mary Magdalen – whose body he had rediscovered here in 1279 – together with an adjoining large monastery. But he also wished to develop around them a sizeable country town, capable of welcoming with its inns, commerce and artisans, the throngs of pilgrims who, since 1279, had grown in numbers. To attract inhabitants, his founding charter of 12 August 1295 specified several advantageous inducements. Nearly all tax burdens were waived. In addition, Charles committed himself to paying the considerable building costs, as well as funding the 'pensions' of the monks, from the royal treasury. It is this which explains the use of the word *royal* in 'Couvent royal'; for – though the adjective is often associated with Louis XII, who brought the monastery under royal protection at the beginning of the sixteenth century – Charles himself did become a few years later on the death of his father, if not 'of France', nevertheless a king.

Begun in 1295, the present basilica acquired today's aspect some 250 years later. Even now its façade and bell tower are unfinished. Yet it remains the largest Gothic building in south-east France, being twenty-nine metres high, seventy-three in length and thirty-seven wide. Charles chose his father's best architect, Pierre d'Agincourt. The original idea was to erect an *aedes vitreas*, a building of glass, rather like the Sainte Chapelle in Paris, built *c.* 1245 by Charles' uncle (St Louis) to house the relics that he had himself assembled. Many stained-glass windows were planned, to give the whole structure a lightness and luminosity. It is not clear whether any of these were ever installed. Whatever the case, none survive and the interior now conveys a different impression than the one intended.

But why such lavish expense on such a massive building in the middle of nowhere? To answer this question, we must look in more detail at the events which took place in 1279.

❧

In 1254, on his return from the seventh crusade, King Louis visited Saint-Maximin, as Joinville – his counsellor and confidant – makes clear in his *Histoire de Saint Louis*. The context of Louis' pilgrimage is itself revealing. He had been absent from his kingdom for six years; the seventh crusade had been a disaster; his brother had been killed in Egypt and he himself taken prisoner. His mother, who had been named Regent during his absence, had died two years previously. The royal fleet, having suffered damage, had been forced to dock at Hyères rather than Aigues-Mortes, the king's port. That he should nonetheless have made the detour to the Sainte-Baume and to Saint-Maximin shows not only his personal devotion to Mary Magdalen but provides further evidence for the continuing fame and popularity of the Provençal sites.

Contrary to what is often stated, there was no actual rivalry or dispute between the monasteries of Vézelay and Saint-Maximin. To begin with, only two or three monks remained at Saint-Maximin and, although they could indicate Mary's empty sarcophagus, neither they nor anyone else knew exactly where her body was hidden, though no local tradition existed of its ever having been removed to Burgundy. We must remember, too, that it was not the monks but Charles, a non-local layman, who insisted on the investigation.

Charles didn't search at random, but went to Aix, to which the Vézelay account pointed and where, as Lieutenant of Provence for his father, he had his palace. There and in the surrounding region he consulted any annals or historical documents available, and also questioned the older inhabitants as to what local tradition might have to say. Everything pointed to the small church at Saint-Maximin, which is described in the accounts of the searches he made as *oratorium, sacrarium, tempulum* or sometimes *ecclesia*. By this was not meant the fifth-century Cassianite priory, but the oratory whose origins dated back to Maximin's time. It had survived the onslaughts of both Charles Martel and the Saracens. It seems that the latter, in keeping with their practice in certain other places, had spared the building so as to collect a special tax from the pilgrims who came to it – in itself, a further indication of the pre-Vézelay origin of the Provençal tradition.

Accordingly, in December 1279 Charles went with his retinue to the place in question. Searches were made in the oratory. What was believed to be Mary's sarcophagus had, of course, been empty for centuries; but all the other tombs were inspected, the walls and floor were probed.

Albanès, in his *Le Couvent royal de Saint-Maximin*, shows that on 8 August 1254 the abbot of Saint-Victor had appointed as prior at Saint-Maximin a certain Maître Adam. Adam was a canon, originally from Tours, who was clerk to Charles' father, Charles I of Anjou and Count of Provence, brother of King Louis. Unlike all previous appointees, not only was he not a monk, he had no connection at all with the mother house of Saint-Victor. To appoint a secular priest to this post was highly unusual and indeed against the monastery's own strict rule, a rule which had been renewed more than once, and would be again in 1269 – by the same abbot. Clearly, on this occasion his hand had been forced – presumably by the Count of Provence, several of whose clerks and chaplains were promoted to high positions.

Significantly, the nomination was made just one month after the visit of Louis to Saint-Maximin and the cave. The situation was now being made official. Not that this out-of-the-way remnant of a monastery seemed to offer promotion! Albanès is surely correct in suggesting that the only explanation for this strange set of circumstances is that, after his visit to the area, the saintly Louis had talked things over with his brother and had suggested to him that he should investigate the Provençal tradition. Although Albanès does not make the connection, it is possible that Louis' comments to the monks at Vézelay (where he was no stranger) regarding his 1254 pilgrimage to Saint-Maximin were influential in their decision to produce and open, after all, their own tomb in 1265.

As for the person to lead such an investigation in Provence, who more appropriate than the Count of Provence himself? The wives of both Louis and Charles – Marguerite of Provence and Beatrice of Provence, respectively – provided a further link with the area. It seems highly likely that they had passed on to their husbands something of its Magdalen traditions. Thus, as an initial move, it seems that Charles had got his own man installed as prior, so as to be free from any local religious authority. However, he was unable to take things any further on account of the many political struggles and battles, at home and abroad, which continuously occupied him. It eventually fell to his son, also called Charles, to take the matter further. In 1278, as his father's Lieutenant, he left the Angevin capital of Naples for Provence. Charles seems in any case to have been more like his saintly uncle than his father. One of his own children would be canonized, as St Louis of Brignoles.

Some political historians can only see in this project the desire of these Angevins to boost their ambitions by having their own patron saint in the heart of their empire – one, moreover, who provided a link with the very Holy Land that they themselves were engaged in attempting to reconquer. Yet even this basest of interpretations shows that, for it to carry conviction, such a Provençal tradition centred on Saint-Maximin must already have existed.

To return to the investigations of 1279, it is repeatedly stated, that the building had been walled in and covered over with earth, as if it had been a crypt. On the contrary, as seen, the chroniclers of the time all call it an *oratorium.*

It was above ground and still served as the church for the handful of monks who lived in the adjacent priory.

After searching in vain for a while, Charles deliberated and then decided to start digging between the tombs that were above ground, and that had already been searched. With renewed energy and excitement the task started, the prince himself joining in. After a while one workman discovered a marble sarcophagus, to the right of the more eminent one in alabaster, which had been Mary's original coffin. As they tried to prise it open, a marvellous odour escaped, such that all those present rushed forward to see what was causing such a strong scent.

It is a phenomenon which is far from being exceptional, even today, in the context of saints' relics, and even icons. Yet it is easy to see why, in this case, they at once thought they might indeed have found the body of Mary Magdalen, she whose precious nard filled the entire house at Bethany with its perfume.

Despite his joy and impatience, Charles ordered that the coffin be closed again and the marble lid secured with his own seal. Any further examination as to what exactly lay inside should wait until such time as this could be done in the proper manner by the appropriate ecclesiastical authorities, duly observed by their civil and legal counterparts. Accordingly, he requested the Bishops of Provence – including Grimier de Vicedominis, Archbishop of Aix, and Bernard de Languisel, Archbishop of Arles – to attend nine days later.

This short delay – understandable if so many important dignitaries were to be assembled – is, in Saxer's eyes, suspicious. He suggests, without the slightest evidence, that Charles was simply giving himself time to devise a 'mise en scène', a 'show'. Time, too, for authenticating documents to be forged.

On the appointed day, Charles' unbroken seal was duly verified and the tomb opened for examination. Inside was an entire body, minus the lower jawbone. Hair was still attached to the skull. Over the left eyebrow there still remained a piece of flesh and skin, which became known as the *Noli me tangere*, after the Gospel verse in which the risen Christ tells Mary not to touch him, the thinking being that he touched her on the forehead at this spot, to stop her from throwing herself at his feet.

This remained attached until well into the eighteenth century, as was verified by different doctors in the course of the various inventories that have been drawn up. For example the medical-legal one of 1640, presided over by Louis de Valois, Count of Artois and Lieutenant-General of Provence, assisted by several learned men including Gassendi of Digne and three doctors. By 1780, when a further inventory was undertaken, it was recorded that it had become loose. It has since then been preserved in a phial and can still be seen in the crypt today.

Perhaps more important was a further discovery. In the dust lay an ancient piece of cork. It had been moved about several times, but then Charles himself happened to notice it. When he picked it up to see what it was, it broke into several pieces. Inside was a small piece of parchment bearing an inscription in Latin.

An official report was drawn up and the tomb then sealed again. Charles requested the attendance of even more dignitaries for the following spring. On 5 May 1280, the prelates of Provence (including the Archbishops of Narbonne, Arles and Aix), many monks and other clergy, counts, barons, and secular officials duly attended.

Absent, however, were the Bishop of Marseilles and the Abbot of Saint-Victor, of which the small priory at Saint-Maximin was still, technically at least, a dependency. Many have been puzzled by this; yet it is probably explained by the bad feeling that lingered on after the externally imposed appointment of outsider Maître Adam as prior.

In the presence of the dignitaries, the body was for the first time solemnly removed from the coffin. At which point a further discovery was made: an object covered in wax (presumably as a means of preservation) and inside a small tablet coated with more wax, on which was written: *Hic requiescit corpus Mariae Magdalenae*. Here lies the body of Mary Magdalen.

There is evidence to suggest that using beeswax in this way was a Provençal custom in early centuries. For example, Faillon quotes from the fifth-century *Life* of St Honoratus, founder of the monastery of Lérins and Archbishop of Arles. St Hilary, his biographer and successor, writes that Honoratus had written a letter of this kind to St Eucherius, Bishop of Lyons, who – alluding to the sweetness of the style and content – replied as follows: 'You have given the beeswax back its honey.'

Charles had commissioned a silver reliquary for the body and, a year later on 25 May 1281, it was duly transferred. For the head, however, a more complex reliquary was ordered in the form of a bust that could be left on permanent display for the benefit of pilgrims. This took some time to complete. (The transfer eventually took place on 10 December 1283, for which occasion Charles' father sent his own crown to be placed atop the reliquary.) Meanwhile Charles kept the head in his palace at Aix. As is stated in documents signed there by the Archbishops of Aix and Arles, he vowed to return the relic to Saint-Maximin when the reliquary was ready – but only on condition that the church there be handed over to the care of 'servants more suited to' the saint's veneration. Otherwise he would place it elsewhere, even if he himself had to build another church. Understandably, Charles cannot have been impressed by Saint-Maximin's rump of a priory – two or three monks in a small run-down building.

Despite the appointment of Maître Adam as prior, the buildings at Saint-Maximin still belonged to Saint-Victor, technically at least. Thus Charles needed papal permission, if he were to carry out his plan of establishing Dominicans there instead. However, political events caused a delay in his plans. In particular, the so-called War of the Sicilian Vespers, which broke out in March 1282, saw him assisting his father in defence of the Angevin interests. On 5 June

1284 he was himself taken prisoner at Messina and held captive in Barcelona.

Having become king while still in captivity (on the death of his father in 1285), he was released three years later. Shortly afterwards, in 1289, he set off for Rome, but events were still against him. Nicolas IV was totally preoccupied with organizing another crusade, before his death in 1292. His successor Celestine V, the hermit who had never wanted to become Pope, was concerned with arranging his own abdication. It was only with the accession of Boniface VIII in 1294 that papal attention was paid to Charles' request.

Charles needed a pope in order to loose what an earlier pope had bound for ever under pain of excommunication. For in the 1040 bull relating to the reconsecration of Saint-Victor, a clause had been inserted against anyone – 'emperor, king, duke, marquis, comte, bishop or archbishop' – who attempted to take over the possessions and property belonging to the monastery. This was understandable after the centuries of invasion, pillage and secular appropriation of these same possessions.

Boniface issued six bulls in a single year, 1295. Three are to do with establishing a Feast, but the others authorized Charles to install Dominicans at Saint-Maximin and the Sainte Baume as guardians of the relics, confirming the break with Saint-Victor that had begun with the appointment of Maître Adam. The Dominicans were a good choice – relatively recently founded, very popular and, like the Franciscans, full of energy. Determined not only to live a life of evangelical piety but dynamically to preach the truth of the Gospel, they seemed to him ideally suited to his vision. In addition, being directly answerable to the Pope, they would be free from interference from the Archbishop of Aix (in whose diocese Saint-Maximin still was) and from the abbot of Saint-Victor.

❧

The originals of the documents drawn up by the ecclesiastical and juridical officials concerning the events of 1279 have been lost. As with most events in history, we only have later copies of what took place drawn up by chroniclers and annalists who were nonetheless reasonably close in time. The two most important are Bernard Gui and Philippe de Cabassole. But what value can be placed on their testimony? Although both were respected for the rigour and honesty of their thought, neither were eyewitnesses.

Bernard Gui (born in Limoges *c.* 1261) was a distinguished Dominican who eventually became Bishop of Lodève. His reputation rests mainly on his qualities as administrator, diplomat and historian. By fastidious work, he collected details of all the events concerning the very many monasteries of his province of Provence, which then stretched from Nice to Bordeaux. In addition, he composed several historical works of considerable value, civil and religious. In particular, he has left to posterity a multitude of information concerning the south of France in the thirteenth and the beginning of the fourteenth century that is to be found nowhere else. He is reputed to have had a highly critical mind and never to have accepted what seemed merely 'probable'.

At one stage, he was close adviser to John XXII in Avignon, for whom he undertook several tricky diplomatic missions. Since Avignon, then, was his base for many years, he was well placed to visit Saint-Maximin and the Sainte Baume. This he did, questioning eyewitnesses and conducting detailed research. No better chronicler, it would seem, could be found than this very shrewd Dominican. It is important to note that, in his account written in 1320, he affirms that he had seen with his own eyes the originals of the two documents found in the coffin.

Very different in style is the account of Philippe de Cabassole, Bishop of Cavaillon, Cardinal, and Petrarch's friend. It is true that he was writing in 1355, some seventy-six years after the events. Yet the very way in which he learned about them was somewhat special. Like Petrarch, Philippe was a close friend of Robert 'the Wise', Charles' son and heir, and it was from him that he heard the tale, on more than one occasion.

As a boy, Robert must have heard the story many a time from his father. The main features will have fixed themselves in his mind from an early age: his father's determination to conduct a thorough investigation among the libraries of Aix; his questioning of the old people; the day in December when, with a small band of workers, he decided to get involved personally. How he had thrown aside his chlamys, his royal cloak, had grabbed some of the workmen's tools, and had set about investigating every nook and cranny of the old oratory. How, finally, he had decided to attack the earthen floor with a pickaxe and spade, the sweat pouring from him. Details like these are what typify an eyewitness account (the eyewitness being Charles himself) and would have impressed themselves upon the mind of a child. Philippe de Cabassole must have felt he was reliving the events, as if he had indeed been present.

None of this, of course, satisfies the critics.

The weight of criticism can be divided into several main charges. Firstly, Mary Magdalen's tomb cannot possibly be in Provence, because it is in Ephesus.

As evidence of this, Launoy and Duchesne quote from Gregory of Tours' *Glory of the Martyrs* (I.29). Gregory was one of the most informed people in the sixth century in the matter of pilgrimages, adds Duchesne, and knew of her tomb. From the sixth century it had become one of the holy places of Ephesus. The claim is repeated by Saxer. *In ea urbe [Ephesus], ut dicitur, Maria Magdalena quiescit, nullum super se tegumen habens.* 'In this town, it is said, Mary Magdalen is buried, although there is no covering over her [tomb].'

Gregory's reference to Mary is unusually short, compared with his normal practice for important saints. Of course, he had never been to Ephesus. He only knew of this tomb, as he himself admits, from the 'Syrian traveller' who helped him transcribe the *Acts* of the Seven Sleepers of Ephesus. Furthermore, the description is itself curious. A saint's body, and such a famous saint, in an uncovered tomb! Nothing is said concerning the date of her burial there or about how, without a covering or some such structure, the tomb was protected not simply from the weather but from profanation. Does it sound like a holy shrine?

Duchesne himself frequently questions Gregory's authority, describing his accounts as often being written with a 'marvellous naivety'. This is true, particularly in connection with his acceptance of certain legends by travellers to the East. For example, the Star of Bethlehem, we are told, is still visible at the bottom of a certain well close to the spot where Christ was born. It seems to be only in the case of Mary Magdalen that, for the purposes of his cause, Duchesne finds Gregory to be infallible.

There exists another document which casts further doubt on the Ephesus hypothesis: a collective letter addressed to Pope Saint Victor by eastern bishops at the end of the second century. They are seeking his permission to continue celebrating the date of Easter according to the tradition they obtained from St John who, as is traditionally believed, settled in Ephesus. In seeking to emphasize the dignity of their local churches, they list the Apostles and other important persons who died in Asia Minor, especially in Ephesus. There is no mention at all of Mary Magdalen. The bishop of Ephesus at the time the letter was written was Polycrates, born in the town twenty-five years after the death of St John. His grandfather could have seen Mary Magdalen with his own eyes, if she had indeed ended her days there. Nor would Polycrates have failed to mention her in the letter. It would have been one of the best recommendations of all.

In 431 Pope Celestine I wrote to the Fathers assembled at Ephesus for the Third Ecumenical Council as follows: 'Let the Apostolic virtues shine forth in the town of Ephesus, where the relics of the holy Evangelist [John] are venerated'. There is no mention of Mary Magdalen. Egeria (or Etheria), who travelled to the Holy Land and to related parts of the Middle East in the fourth century, writes of how keen she was 'to go to Ephesus in Asia, for the sake of prayer, because of the memorial of the holy and blessed Apostle John'. Again, no mention of Mary.

Strangely, when it suits, such arguments from silence are very dear to the critics. The fact, for example, that Gregory nowhere mentions Mary Magdalen as having come to Provence is considered to be adequate proof that she did not come. This, even though Gregory himself says on more than one occasion that his compilation is not meant to be exhaustive, and that he is mainly concerned with saints not yet written about. Eusebius of Caesarea – the early fourth-century Father of Church History – nowhere describes Mary as having died in the East. In fact, he never mentions her at all. If the argument from silence is to be rigorously adhered to, we might conclude from this that she did not.

Launoy, followed by Duchesne, also lays store by a reference made in a homily by Modestus, Patriarch of Jerusalem in the early seventh century – that is, as quoted by Photius, Patriarch of Constantinople, two centuries later. Yet Photius' text is puzzling:

> Magdalen from whom the Saviour drove out seven demons was throughout her life a virgin, and in the account of her martyrdom it is said that because of her perfect virginity and excellent purity, she seemed to her executioners like limpid crystal. [. . .] Having become chief of the disciples, on account of her purity and the love she had for the Saviour, Magdalen was surnamed Mary, like his divine [sic] Mother.

The internal contradictions here are self-evident. Firstly, there is the possibility, at least, of an inconsistency between having 'seven demons' and yet displaying perpetual virginity. Even the explanation of the name – with its confusion between 'name' and 'surname' – contradicts the Gospels, which describe her as 'Mary who is called Magdalen' (Luke 8:2). Again, does any other source inform us that Mary Magdalen suffered martyrdom? Is there, perhaps, confusion here with some other holy woman also called Magdalen?

Why, one wonders, do the critics – who are so industrious in dismantling any pro-Provençal text – unquestioningly believe what Photius claims to have been written by Modestus? As Saxer himself stresses, the cult of saints tends to develop first where they are buried. Why, then, has there never been for Ephesus any well-attested, early, constant tradition such as that in Provence?

Interestingly, Escudier writes of how the shock caused by Launoy's assertions in the seventeenth century provoked a consultation of Greek monks in Cyprus (where some say that Lazarus is buried). These replied (according to an entry in the *Acta Sanctorum* for 22 July) that it had been a constant and ancient tradition among them that, though he had spent time in Cyprus, Lazarus had later travelled to Provence and was buried there with Martha and Mary.

❧

The second focus of criticism concerns the text of the longer document found in the sarcophagus, which translates as follows:

> In the year 710 of the Nativity of the Lord, the 6th day of December, secretly in the night, in the reign of the most pious Eudes, King of the Franks, in the period of the ravages caused by the perfidious nation of Saracens, this body of the most dear and venerable Saint Mary Magdalen was, through fear of the said perfidious nation, transferred from her alabaster tomb into this one of marble, after having removed from it the body of Sidonius, since it would be better hidden there.

The sceptics take it for granted that this is a forgery slipped into the coffin at an opportune moment. Yet are we to accept that the archbishops, bishops, other prelates, lawyers, municipal officers and the rest were all party to a fraud, or that they were all taken in? Apparently so. Saxer suggests, quite gratuitously, that it was one of the prelates present on 18 December who let a forged document fall into the coffin from the sleeve of his ecclesiastical garment. If it were not one of the prelates, he continues, it could have been Charles himself, or one of his counsellors.

Was it perhaps, as has also been suggested, the handful of monks from Saint-Victor still in residence at the time of the discovery who had perpetrated a fraud? Had Charles colluded with them? If so, upon learning that they were to be replaced by Dominicans for their trouble, they would soon have made the truth known!

Regarding the text itself, the critics suggest that several things ring false: the dating system; the phrase 'anno Nativitatis Dominicae'; the reference to Saracens; and the reference to Eudes.

Duchesne claims that in 710 the system of dating from the Incarnation was not known in France, especially in the south. It was only introduced, he says, after Bede had used it in his *Ecclesiastical History* of 735. Others claim, however, that it was used in England before Bede's time, in charters drawn up by Anglo-Saxon kings. In France, too, evidence exists for an earlier use. Bérenger, in his *Sainte Marie-Madeleine en Provence*, refers to the *Nouveau traité de diplomatique* and *L'Art de vérifier les dates* (both by Benedictine scholars) where mention is made of an act of donation made to the cathedral of Saint Bénigne in Dijon, dated *anno ab Incarnatione Domini DCXXXII* (632). Moreover, as is well known, the era of the Incarnation was introduced in Italy as early as 525 by Denis the Small. It spread to France in the seventh century, though it is true that it did not become well established until the eighth.

As for the precise phrase *anno Nativitatis Dominicae*, Duchesne claims that this only came into use long after the eighth century. Bérenger, on the other hand, shows that the above reference books again make it clear that – though there was no uniformity, some documents counting from the Annunciation, for example – reckoning the beginning of the year from the Nativity was not unusual by the end of the eighth century. He cites an example found in the records of the abbey of Saint Bertin, at St Omer: *Anno ejusdem regis qui erat annus Dominicae Nativitatis DCCLXXVIII* (778).

Turning his attention to the Saracens (i.e. the North African Moslems), Duchesne asserts that in 710 they were still in Africa, so fear of them was rather premature. Yet the first maritime attacks on Spain took place, if unsuccessfully, in 675. In 698 Carthage was captured. In 710 Tangiers fell and Ceuta attacked, a town considered to be the key to Spain and Europe. By April of the next year 7,000 men had disembarked on the mainland. In 712 Cordoba and Seville were taken. Progress was so rapid that, by the beginning of 713, nearly every town in the Pyrenees had a Moslem government. The Bibliothèque Nationale in Paris houses a collection of Saracen coins struck in Spain, of which one is dated 710 and two 711.

The Provençals would have known of these developments; they might even have feared an invasion from the sea, of the sort which later did indeed take place. Furthermore, the word 'invasion' is not used in the text, nor is 'Provence'. Indeed, the 'period of ravages' that is cited might refer not to the immediately surrounding area, but to the south of France – including the south-west – in general. It might even have been a reference to European Christendom as a whole, including Spain.

Nor did the Provençals need to wait for news from the west, for trade between Marseilles and the Orient was still thriving. The main merchants and tradesmen of the time were the 'Syrians' – as active in this respect as the Dutch in the seventeenth century. Surely the word would have spread that, from the 630s, the Holy Land had been overrun. Long before 710, Egypt had in turn been invaded and with it Alexandria, another port with which Marseilles traded regularly. Nearer to home, Sicily had fallen in the 660s.

Throughout Provence in the early eighth century the bodies of saints and other relics were being displaced and hidden. The martyrdom of St Porcaire (Porcarius) and 500 monks not long after 710, on the island of Lérins, proves that the fears of the monks of Saint-Maximin were not fanciful. Porcaire is said to have had warnings in dreams that this would happen and that he should hide the monastery's treasured relics. Interestingly, it is now known that in Spain several votive crowns which had been offered to Visigothic kings had been hastily buried, when news of the Moslem incursions began to spread. The Saint-Maximin relics only had to wait until the thirteenth century before being unearthed again; the Visigothic votive crowns were not discovered by archaeologists until the nineteenth.

Duchesne wonders why a switch from one coffin to another would fool any Saracens. Would they, he asks, be able to distinguish between the best relics? Yet, surely, they would be looking in tombs, not for any bones (sacred or otherwise) but for treasure. The most expensive-looking tomb – namely, the one in which Mary had until 710 lain, the one most prominently displayed – would certainly have been the one to attract their attention. The monks, for their part, would have wished to avoid any defilement of their most prized relic, even if this only involved a rummaging and ransacking. Even today the average householder is free to insure what is of value to him personally, regardless of whether a theoretical burglar might share his opinion.

Such exchanges between tombs, far from being unusual, must have been made on countless occasions down the ages. One example from the time of the Revolution might serve as evidence. During the upheavals, the church of St Agricola at Avignon was profaned. However – as can be read in the *Vie de Saint Agricol* by a local lawyer, Augustin Canron – the parish priest, the Abbé Pignatelli, had taken the precaution of hiding the relics of the town's patron saint at the bottom of another common or garden tomb, nearby in the choir.

❧

The final criticism concerns the identity of Eudes. Duchesne asks:

> Who is this Odoin who is described as King of the Franks? No king of this name is found anywhere in the long list of Kings of France. There is no question of it being King Eudes who reigned from 888 to 896, for in his time Provence was subject to Louis [the Blind]. Claims have also been made for Eudes (Eudo), Duke of Aquitaine, who never bore the title *Rex Francorum* and never exercised any authority whatsoever beyond the Rhône, from which he was separated by the Visigothic province of Septimania. Moreover, the name Eudo is not equivalent to Odoinus. No contemporary would have made such an error.

On the other hand, Bérenger again cites the authors of the *Nouveau traité de diplomatique*, who clearly state that 'the names Odoinus, Odo, Eudes, Odoin, Odon, Odoic are simply variants of the same name and Odoin, Roi des Francs, is the same person as Eudes, Duke of Aquitaine'. They continue by adding that he was in fact recognized by King Chilperic II (of Neustria) as sovereign of the whole of Aquitaine, the ancient Kingdom of Toulouse, precisely the part of the country nearest to an already conquered Spain. It was Eudes who later was to fight the Saracens and stop their advance at Toulouse in 721. For this he received gifts from the Pope, which proves his independence in foreign relations. Moreover, at the time there was sometimes a blurring of distinctions between such titles as 'duke' and 'king'.

Eudes – sometimes called Odo the Great in modern encyclopaedias – was certainly in power by 700 and reigned until 735, over the lands situated between the Loire, the Ocean, the Pyrenees, Septimania and well beyond the Rhône into what we know as Provence, despite what Duchesne says. Ancient historians, foreign as well as French, not only gave him the title of King, but indicate that charters were dated according to the years of his reign. Is it surprising, then, that he was given the title King, not of France, but of the Franks?

Saxer continued to maintain that the supposed forger had in mind the ninth-century Eudes, since the expression *rex francorum* was only used, he claimed, by the Carolingians. Yet the *Encyclopédie Universelle* contains an article on the (earlier) Merovingian dynasty – to which Eudes is believed to have belonged – in which we read that 'every Merovingian sovereign bore the title *rex francorum* which asserted that, over and above the different territorial lands, there existed a unity (the *Regnum*)'.

From the ninth to the seventeenth century not just Eudes' royalty but his very existence was ignored. The inscription at Saint-Maximin, for this reason alone, must be at least older than the ninth century. Any thirteenth-century forger who expected to be believed would surely not have introduced the name of a person whose very existence was unknown to the historians of his day.

❧

Beyond supposing that it too was secreted into the coffin, the critics do not discuss the shorter document. Perhaps because they fear that its very brevity suggests its authenticity: *Hic requiescit corpus Mariae Magdalenae.* 'Here lies the body of Mary Magdalen.' As Le Blant points out, in his *Inscriptions Chrétiennes de la Gaule*, the most complicated funerary inscriptions are the most recent. Thus, from 469 he lists as evidence *hic requiescit in pace*; by 473 this becomes *hic requiescit bonae memoriae*; and by 488 *hic requiescit in pace bonae memoriae.* It would seem that the even shorter Saint-Maximin *hic requiescit* dates, then, from the first half of the fifth century, as does the sarcophagus, and was most probably written on the occasion of the transfer of the body from its original, primitive coffin.

It will be recalled that this shorter text was written on a tablet coated with wax. Would a thirteenth-century forger have been aware of this very ancient custom?

All in all, whatever one thinks of the above evidence, whatever one thinks of the critics' objections, one question remains. Why did Charles' discovery in Provence in 1279 result almost immediately in the collapse of the Burgundian claim? Vézelay – despite its magnificent site and church, its widely promulgated version of the Magdalen story, its hundred-year association with the high and mighty of all Europe – fell swiftly from grace. Saint-Maximin – a huddle of humble buildings in an out-of-the-way plain – more or less at once became the sole focus of attention. Why did the Burgundian monks seemingly acquiesce so meekly? Why did Christians of all estates immediately accept the fact that Mary's body had after all never been removed from Provence, when received opinion for over a century had told them that it had. Even if 1279 had been an elaborate fraud, these questions remain unanswered.

As for frauds, it seems that in the minds of many people today, this is what relics automatically are. Before looking in more detail, then, at what Charles might have unearthed, we should perhaps digress for a moment.

9

A Short Excursus on Relics

The use of relics by Christians has often had a bad press, not only in the popular media but among those scholars who only see in them evidence of superstition or a means of securing prestige, protection or profit. Cases of such malpractice have, of course, existed from the earliest times. Yet – as can be seen from the writings of Augustine and Cassian, among many others – these have always been fiercely denounced. Furthermore, as the saying goes, *abusus non tollit usus*. Abuse does not invalidate legitimate use. The Piltdown hoax does not invalidate archaeology. Nor does Watergate invalidate democracy. On the contrary. Similarly, the existence of forged religious relics does not remove the possibility of there being genuine ones. To begin with, we must allow that things from long ago *do* survive. Our museums are full, for example, of Egyptian items at least twice as ancient as anything claimed by Christians.

If, then, genuine Christian relics do exist, why are they valued?

They are, of course, never worshipped but simply honoured or venerated. Nor are they a medieval innovation. Yet, living as we do in a culture over-influenced by the Enlightenment, many people – Christians among them – seem not to realize that the rationale of relics is inextricably bound up with Christianity's basic doctrines of Creation, Incarnation and Resurrection. In fact, it can be said without exaggeration that their veneration derives directly, not from any primitive superstition but from an extremely advanced theology of the body and of matter in general.

For Christians, the material creation is neither evil, unreal, contingent nor a barrier between man and Creator. It is essentially 'very good', as Genesis insists (1:31). Secondly, since at the Incarnation the second Person of the Trinity – 'through Whom all things were created', as the Creed makes clear – took, not just a human soul but human flesh, matter itself was in him 'saved', renewed, restored. We can never let up our guard in fighting against a dualistic interpretation of Christianity, which would reduce it to being merely a programme of moral regeneration or, perhaps worse still, a branch of Gnosticism. This is to overlook its truly material, indeed cosmic, significance; to forget that we look forward, as Paul puts it (Romans 8:21), to the day when 'creation itself will be set free from its bondage to decay'. Nor should we forget that after Christ's Ascension (and after Mary's bodily Assumption) matter has *already* been taken up into Heaven.

For orthodox Christianity, man is not simply a body, nor is he simply a soul. He is certainly not a soul imprisoned in a body, though much popular religious language – 'save our souls', for example – can in this respect be misleading. Rather, he is a unity of body and soul, a psychosomatic whole. As St Thomas Aquinas put it, commenting on 1 Corinthians 15: 'The soul is not the whole man and my soul is not me'. When St Paul contrasts flesh and spirit, he is making the same point; for by 'flesh' he simply means the *whole* man in his fallen state, and by 'spirit' the *whole* man in so far as he is redeemed.

Orthodox Christianity maintains that the body is redeemed and sanctified along with the soul. It is already the temple of the Holy Spirit and will some day be conformed to the glorious body of the risen Christ. Thus, since the body will rise again, albeit in a modified state, it is fitting that respect should be shown for the bodily remains of the saints.

❧

Regarding the remains of Mary Magdalen, as with other saints, misunderstandings can easily arise – if all the claimed relics are totalled up – as to the number of legs, arms, fingers or indeed bodies she may have possessed. Yet even when false claims have been discounted, we must not forget that an 'arm', a 'leg', a 'finger' or even a 'body' might in reality have originally meant no more than a minute fragment of the same. It is conceivable that, with the course of time, people could in all honesty have come to mistake the whole for the part. Those sceptics too eager to bring mathematics to their aid have been misled by ignoring this fact. In these days of holograms and DNA testing, it should be obvious that such dismemberment and cutting up poses no theological problem.

Many of the relics of Mary Magdalen claimed by other places will without doubt have come from Saint-Maximin. High-ranking persons frequently used their prestige to persuade the monks to part with a small portion. So many pieces had been given away by the end of the fifteenth century that in 1495 Charles VIII, King of Sicily and Count of Provence, was obliged to issue a solemn edict forbidding any such practice.

❧

In 1793, when the revolutionaries ransacked the church, the relics were plundered and thrown about, since the looters were only interested in the gold and the jewels. The intrepid sacristan, Joseph Bastide, managed to save the head and a few other items. These were hidden throughout the Terror, according to local historian Solange Rostan, in the house of one J. B. Sudre. Similarly a Madame Ricard de Seoult managed to retrieve the lower third of the right tibia and a lock of hair. In the autumn of 1794, whilst a refugee at Bonnieux in the Vaucluse, she left these items for safekeeping with those who had been sheltering her, the grandparents of Monseigneur Terris. Monseigneur Terris in turn bequeathed them to the Archbishop of Fréjus (to whose diocese Saint-Maximin and the Sainte Baume were now assigned). On Mary's feast day in 1890, these were placed in the grotto.

As soon as the troubles had passed, a modest reliquary was made in 1798, thanks to the generosity of several farmers. When, in 1804, the first post-revolutionary inventory was drawn up, it was confirmed that few of the original items had survived. Nevertheless, the rescued skull was eventually placed in a new gilded bronze bust-reliquary, paid for by public subscription. In 1860 in pouring rain, 10,000 people gathered for the transfer of the skull to its new home. Lacordaire – whose book on Mary Magdalen had just been published – was sadly too ill to attend. The basilica was still in the state of advanced depredation in which the revolutionary period had left it. Only the thousands of candles held by the faithful – 'tout est en feu', said the papers – imparted a festive air. It is the same bust-reliquary that we see today. Since it is in need of renovation, a new appeal has been launched.

❦

In 1781 Louis XVI had given a femur to Don Ferdinand, Duke of Parma and Infant of Spain. It was later returned and in 1824 donated to the church of La Madeleine in Paris. In 1974, this – and the remaining relics from Saint-Maximin and the Sainte Baume – were subjected to an examination by experts from the *Institut d'Archéologie Méditerranéenne*. Regrettably, they were not carbon-dated. When applied to bones, the process apparently destroys a large proportion of the original material. Moreover, any attempt was rendered pointless by the realization that the bones had been protected with wax. Yet this in itself brings to mind the tablet similarly covered with wax that Charles found in the coffin in 1279, bearing the inscription *Hic requiescit corpus Mariae Magdalenae*. This had presumably been put there in 710, when the body was transferred to the tomb of Sidonius for safety. That is, if it did not date back even further, to the fourth century, when the body was removed from its primitive coffin and placed in its white sarcophagus.

Although it was not possible scientifically to say whether all the bones belonged to the same person, they all *were* those of a woman of about fifty, short, slender, and of a typically Mediterranean type. In short, there is nothing that would obviously rule them out from being what the tradition claims them to be.

10

Face to Face with the Skull

When you consult the plan in the pale blue leaflet that can be bought for a few pence at the entrance of the basilica, it becomes clear that the small crypt reputedly containing Mary Magdalen's sarcophagus is almost exactly in the centre. Undeniably, the entire building has been erected around it, as one vast 'casket' or shrine. Right by the steps to the crypt is the magnificent eighteenth-century pulpit, into whose burnished walnut are carved some of the most attractive depictions of Mary, surpassing in elegance most statues or paintings. Its position is symbolic, reminding us that she was the first preacher of the good news of the Resurrection, lynchpin of the faith.

The first short flight of steps leads to a landing, before the final descent. The walls are covered with graffiti but, like that inside the porch and on the various pillars, of the sort that you want to decypher. Handsome calligraphy; intriguing dates (1840, 1691); indications of origin ('Tourangeau' for someone from the Touraine); descriptions of the person's trade (*plâtrier*, for example); and several of the familiar 'horseshoe' marks that can be seen throughout this basilica as well as in various places on the Sainte-Baume. Do they, too, represent a trade? That of blacksmith? There seem to be too many for that. They are more likely to be a stylized representation of the grotto. For it is certainly the case that these ancient inscriptions have been made by *Compagnons* of old, as they made their obligatory pilgrimage. Some see in the 'horseshoe' an echo of a fertility symbol, a reminder of the grotto's ancient association with pagan rites.

But what does this crypt contain? According to Duchesne, any objective observer will conclude that it is nothing other than the burial vault of a rich Gallo-Roman family of the fifth or sixth century. Not unlike, he adds, the similar monument at La Gayole near Brignoles, some 12 kilometres away.

Yet Duchesne never came to Saint-Maximin, despite the request made by the Dominicans of his day, and never personally saw its crypt or its sarcophagi. Neither did he visit La Gayole. If he had, he would have seen that the two sites are totally different. Moreover, if it had simply been a matter of inventing a legend based on a suitable tomb, why had those responsible not chosen the one at La Gayole? Dating from the third or even second century, it is the oldest known Christian tomb in France even today. Furthermore, it is the chapel at La Gayole, not the one at Saint-Maximin, that is frequently mentioned in the documents relating to the renaissance of Saint-Victor during the eleventh and twelfth centuries – precisely the time when, according to the critics, the legend was being developed.

If Duchesne's opinion is correct, one wonders why – contrary to contemporary practice, as can be seen at Les Alyscamps in Arles – not a single inscription can be found on the medallions or escutcheons of any of the sarcophagi. If this had been the private burial place of a Gallo-Roman family, even a Christianized one, it must obviously have been wealthy. Yet there is not a word to refer to the names of any of their loved ones.

❧

Terribile est videre hanc faciam.

'Awesome it is to look upon this face.' So wrote the German Jerôme Münzer in his diary account of the pilgrimage he made in the 1490s. It is indeed the golden bust reliquary, at the far end of the small vaulted chamber, with its skull and staring eye-sockets that first attracts your attention. There are four coffins in all. Three from the fourth century, one from the fifth. Whose were they?

The Provençal tradition claims that these are the tombs of St Maximin, St Sidonius, the so-called Holy Innocents, and Mary Magdalen herself. The latter, on which the skull reliquary rests and which has been dated to the fourth century, has been made into an altar. It is so badly damaged that nothing now enables us to identify it as being unequivocally that of Mary, with the possible exception of the quality of the stone. It would be a rare choice, even for a rich Roman matron. Contrary to what might be imagined, however, it was not the revolutionaries of 1793 who damaged it, but simply the long stream of pilgrims down the centuries. Some of these – probably from the late Middle Ages onwards – seem to have been intent on taking home a chip, either out of misplaced piety, as a fetish or lucky charm, or simply as a memento. Rather as people salvaged chunks of the Berlin Wall when it was finally demolished. The German pilgrim Münzer proudly admits to having left with a sizeable chunk, handed to him by the prior himself! In 1634 it is known that, since the damage caused had become so considerable, a wooden defensive barrier was erected.

One scene on the front depicts Pilate washing his hands. Pilate – whose head is no longer whole – is seated, wearing a buckled *paludamentum*, or military cloak. Behind him a slave carries a ewer, long since chipped off, as is the bowl into which the water is poured. All that can now be made out are what remains of the tripod that supported the bowl. Some critics have claimed that it was a mistaken identification of this scene – namely, that it represents Mary Magdalen bringing her vase of ointment to Christ – that lies at the heart of the legend, whether or not this was fabricated in good faith. There is, of course, absolutely no evidence to support this hypothesis, no reference to any such identification anywhere in the tradition.

As the other sarcophagi in the crypt still do, the one associated with Mary originally had a frieze. This seems to have completely disappeared by about the sixteenth century – most likely as a result of the 'holy vandalism' discussed earlier. Such a frieze, free-standing and protruding upwards, would have been the most vulnerable part of all. However, we know from ancient accounts that the scenes carved on it *did* specifically concern her and thus did seem to identify this tomb as hers. There were apparently six in all: Mary in the house of the Pharisee; performing the anointing at Bethany; hastening to the tomb, carrying ointment; accosting the 'gardener'; throwing herself at Jesus' feet; announcing the Resurrection to the Apostles.

These scenes are listed in *The Golden Legend* and in Vézelay's account. Yet even those writers, such as Gui and Cabassole, who disagreed with Vézelay's claim did not correct its version on this point. And they had both visited the crypt themselves. (It will be recalled that the *Ancienne Vie* from the fifth or sixth century had already made it clear that on the tomb was a carving of Mary bathing Christ's feet with her tears in the house of Simon.) Gislebert Crispin (d.1117), abbot of Westminster Abbey, even referred to this frieze in support of his belief in the unity of the three women. The existence of such a frieze would show that by the fourth century – long before the time of Gregory the Great (d.604), who is too often blamed for originating this idea – the belief that the three were one had become so established as literally to be set in stone.

Much has been written about this stone. Duchesne saw here evidence to support his negative assessment. As seen, the document found by Charles in 1279 states that Mary's body was transferred from an alabaster coffin to one of marble. Duchesne claims, as does Saxer, that the fraudsters tripped themselves up, since none of the coffins at Saint-Maximin are of alabaster.

Or are they?

Duchesne admits that this particular sarcophagus, though marble, is of a very fine grain that might be mistaken for alabaster. Any visitor can see at once that the material from which it has been made is indeed distinctive, different from that of the other three. Moreover, even today, the use of the term 'alabaster' is less than clear-cut. One Egyptologist has even found it necessary to write an article entitled 'The misuse of the term "alabaster"'.

Confusingly, 'alabaster' is a name applied to two very different minerals: gypsum and calcite. Alabaster proper, according to today's usage, is a fine-grained variety of gypsum. However, when the ancients used the term, they were normally referring to the calcite variety – 'Oriental alabaster', as it is sometimes called. To be accurate, this is a misnomer, for it is actually a type of marble. However, it was used by the Egyptians and Romans for sarcophagi. It was also highly prized for the making of perfume bottles and ointment vases, which were as a result called *alabastra*. This is precisely the word used by Matthew, Mark and Luke to describe the container carried by Mary in the Pharisee's house and at Bethany. In choosing this distinctive, finer quality of marble for just one of the tombs at Saint-Maximin, did those responsible – possibly the first Cassianites – have this Gospel vocabulary in mind? If they did, the material itself – regardless of any sculpted scenes it might have contained – would serve to underline the identity of its occupant.

Technically, then, the milky white sarcophagus believed to be Mary's may well be marble; but can we be surprised that the 710 document referred (in good faith) to a tomb of 'alabaster'? It seems that Duchesne and Saxer, not for the first time, have jumped to their conclusion too hastily.

Cut into thin sheets, this so-called alabaster is translucent enough to be used for small windows. It was precisely this translucent quality that was vividly brought home to a certain Marcel Chappe, whom I saw describing his experience on one of Philippe's videos. He was relating something that had taken place in 1930, when he was still a young man; but by his manner and expression, it might have happened yesterday. He had gone down into the crypt one day to pay his respects. There he happened to find workmen engaged in restoration. Seeing that he was interested in Mary's tomb, they offered to show him how fine its material was. They lit a candle and placed it inside. To his amazement he could see, quite distinctly and from the outside, the halo formed by the glow.

When analysed, the stone, though marble, was discovered to be of a highly prized white variety, from the eastern half of the Empire. Either from the imperial quarries on the island of Proconnesus (nowadays known as Marmara in the sea of the same name, near Constantinople) or from Dokimeion (in Phrygia). Today's archaeologists agree that it is of eastern provenance.

A further significant feature was discovered by accident in 1904, when work was undertaken following an incursion by thieves. Mary's sarcophagus had to be moved, revealing for the first time in many decades, possibly centuries, the side facing the wall. In it was discovered a small square opening. Experts agree that this is a *fenestella*, a telltale sign that the coffin did contain the body of a saint, even if it were not that of Mary Magdalen. Through such openings pilgrims would insert some small object or a piece of cloth which, once it had touched the remains of the saint, would itself become sanctified and considered as a relic. Gregory of Tours describes such a practice taking place at the tomb of St Peter in the Vatican.

If such a *fenestella* had been made, it was self-evidently intended to be used. At some time in the past – presumably in or shortly after the fourth century, to which the sarcophagus has been dated – what is now the rear side must therefore have been accessible to the faithful. This is precisely what the *Vie Primitive* from the fifth or sixth century seems to suggest, when it describes it as being 'on display' in the church Maximin erected for it.

One might wonder why sarcophagi from the fourth and fifth century should contain the bodies of people who died in the first. This presents no problem. Few early Christians could afford expensive monuments; and even for those who could, the reality of brutal persecution fostered discretion. Believers were buried humbly and simply until Constantine's establishment of Christianity as the official religion. The bodies of revered people, of saints, would then be reinterred in much grander fashion. In addition, it was often the case that sarcophagi were reused, as was the one referred to by Duchesne at La Gayole. That sarcophagus was manufactured in the second or third century, but a later engraving shows that it was reused for a rich Christian woman named Syagria in the fifth century.

It is perfectly reasonable to suggest that this could have happened with the bodies of Maximin and Mary Magdalen. Indeed, the various excavations and digs that have been undertaken support this. In looking at their findings, we shall also discover proof that what we have been calling the 'crypt' – and which today is precisely that – was for over a thousand years a building that stood above ground.

❧

The installation of the town's main drainage system in the 1960s accidentally revealed the presence of many tombs, dating from the fifth to the tenth century, all orientated towards the present crypt. This in itself suggests that a saint was buried there. If not Mary Magdalen or Maximin, then who?

In 1993 when various road works were being undertaken in the immediate vicinity of the basilica, archaeologists Jean Guyon, Michel Fixot and François Carrazé were permitted to undertake an investigation. The report of their findings makes interesting reading. An initial examination revealed the existence of an ancient baptistery. This justified a further, longer period of exploration, which took place over four months, from April to July in 1994.

It was discovered that, next to the baptistery and communicating with it by means of three doors, was a building some ten metres long, which had been restored at least twice. It was identified as a religious building from the fifth century. Further investigation of the baptistery showed that its layout and design resembled a sixth-century baptistery at Aix, Maximin's episcopal seat. A similar date is proposed for this one. It was already known that other rural churches in the south-east of France had such baptisteries adjoining a church, but the archaeologists were surprised by the size of that at Saint-Maximin. While smaller than the ones at Marseilles and Aix, it nonetheless equals in size those at the episcopal centres of Riez and Fréjus.

To the north and south, evidence was found of several annexes. All in all, it is clear that here was an unusually stable group of religious buildings of considerable importance and that remained in continuous use, with modifications, until the time when Charles undertook his own building project in 1295. It also became evident that the archaeologists had only begun to scratch the surface. Two further exploratory investigations, made in 1996 in the Place de l'Hôtel de Ville next to the basilica, revealed the existence of a building with three apses, which would suggest a church typical of the age of Constantine of the sort commonly found around the Mediterranean. Similar, in fact, to the restored fifth-century Chapelle de la Pépiole at Six-Fours-les-Plages, some 50 kilometres south of Saint-Maximin, not far from Toulon.

To return to the question of the 'crypt', this is a perfect example of the frequent erroneousness of 'received opinion'. As is now clear, there is no archaeological support for its having been a vault, that is, an underground building. It was unquestionably part and parcel of the entire complex. The baptistery and other religious buildings discovered were almost three metres below present ground level, that is, at precisely the same level as the 'crypt'. Moreover, you do not need to be an archaeologist to work out that, in order to enter the basilica today, from the level of the streets leading to the west façade, you must first ascend several metres up the steps provided.

That Charles should have erected a new church *on top of*

the earlier one, instead of first demolishing it, was not in itself a unique occurrence – particularly if the older building was of special significance. In fact, the very same thing had happened at Saint-Victor, when it rose from its ashes in the second half of the tenth century. There the energetic abbot Ysarn built an upper church on top of the ancient *martyrium* and its associated buildings, which then – exactly like the Saint-Maximin *oratorium* – became the crypt.

All in all, these recent archaeological discoveries leave one wondering. Why would a relatively extensive and important complex of religious buildings – let alone the specially orientated graves – have grown up around this out-of-the-way 'crypt', if it had merely been the funeral chamber of a rich family who farmed the vast agricultural plain? There may be a perfectly simple non-Magdalenian answer. Yet the critics do not even ask the question.

I had been discussing these archaeological findings with Philippe, when he asked me whether I had read the book by Father Valatx, the Dominican responsible for the basilica in the 1920s. I replied that as yet I hadn't. In fact, his *La Basilique de Saint-Maximin La Sainte-Baume* (1927) is not so easy to track down.

'Well, when you do get a chance,' Philippe continued, raising his index finger, 'you will see that he documents a much earlier discovery that not many people know about.'

This took place in 1859. Preparations were under way for a solemn celebration to mark the translation on 20 May 1860 of the skull from its post-Revolutionary makeshift reliquary to the one we see today. It was decided to take the opportunity to renovate the stone slabs. As things progressed, the workmen were considerably surprised to discover, 50cm below the surface, three primitive tombs from the first or second century. At the time, so busy were the authorities with preparing for the celebrations, that inadequate notice was taken of this. Fortunately, Father Valatx recorded the discovery, which took place during the time of one of his predecessors, Father Vian. Two of the tombs were in the centre of the crypt, a metre apart; the third under the sarcophagus of St Sidonius.

Whose were they? For, apart from a very small box of bones nestling amidst masonry rubble in one of them, all three were empty. The bodies they contained must at some time have been transferred elsewhere. This information explained a detail that had been puzzling me for a while. I had noticed that into the stone floor of the crypt had been carved two crosses. No book seemed to mention them; few people had even noticed them – not even Philippe. Yet, clearly they must mark the position of the two central tombs.

'What do you think?' asked Philippe. 'Could they have been the original coffins of Mary, Maximin and Sidonius? Before they were placed, after Constantine's legalization of Chrisianity, in the grander ones we see today?'

Such a transfer was not uncommon, once persecution had ceased for good, the most notable example being that of St Peter in Rome. Moreover, it should not be forgotten that – in the opinion of experts such as Le Blant and Revoil – the crypt is older than Mary's fourth-century sarcophagus. It has been renovated and altered on more than occasion, most obviously – though not most recently – when the present-day basilica was built. The niche at the far end, where Mary's coffin and skull reliquary are kept, is thought to be one of the still visible older parts.

'Another thing . . .' Philippe paused for a second. 'Well, it makes you wonder how much else lies underground. Under the basilica, the municipal buildings, the streets and the squares.'

Indeed.

What the latest archaeological findings seem to support is the belief that the present-day crypt is none other than the small oratory built by Maximin, possibly as a missionary outpost, at a crossroads in this rich agricultural area. Whether or not Mary ever spent time up at the cave, the tradition says that it was here that she received the viaticum from Maximin, and here that she died and was buried.

Awesome it is to enter this place!

Crypt of the Basilica, with Mary’s sarcophagus and skull reliquary at the far end.

Epilogue

Exactitude is not truth
(Matisse)

An unquestionably important feature of the Provençal tradition concerning Mary Magdalen is the role played by memory. It is memory, against all the odds, that has helped keep the legend alive and helped it to be handed down, in the root meaning of the word 'tra-dition', from generation to generation. As the celebrated historian of religion Mircea Eliade remarked, primitive legends are veritable libraries of culture. In themselves they constitute a historical document. Sir Arthur Quiller-Couch expressed a similar point of view, when he pointed out that a legend, however exaggerated upon fact, is its own fact. Moreover, the celebrated Bollandist H. Delehaye himself admitted, in his *Les Légendes hagiographiques*, that a legend 'of necessity has a historical or topographical connection. It presupposes an historical fact, which is its subject or pretext'. We might add that legends often point to the deeper meaning of historical facts. Yet, as for objective proof in such cases, the difficulties were made clear as early as the third century by Origen, in Book 1 of his *Contra Celsum*:

> Before we begin our reply, we have to remark that the endeavour to show, with regard to almost any history, however true, that it actually occurred, and to produce an intelligent conception regarding it, is one of the most difficult undertakings that

> can be attempted, and is in some instances an impossibility. For suppose that someone were to assert that there never had been any Trojan war, chiefly on account of the impossible narrative interwoven therewith, about a certain Achilles being the son of a sea-goddess Thetis and of a man Peleus, or Sarpedon being the son of Zeus, or Ascalaphus and Ialmenus the sons of Ares, or Aeneas that of Aphrodite, how should we prove that such was the case, especially under the weight of the fiction attached, I know not how, to the universally prevalent opinion that there really was a war in Ilium between Greeks and Trojans?

To return to memory, however, its task is made easier in those places where sacred and secular celebrations still mingle or, indeed, merge. So it is with the festivities around the feast day of Mary Magdalen at Saint-Maximin. Other villages in these parts may claim her as their patron. In fact, she is the official patron saint of the whole of Provence, which perhaps explains why, traditionally, many girls were named after her, often preferring the diminutive form Manon. The eponymous heroine of Pagnol's *Manon des Sources* is a case in point. But nowhere are the celebrations grander than at Saint-Maximin, where they last for five days.

There are, of course, the usual fairground attractions. To watch the taller ones being erected in the side streets, in and amongst the spreading branches of the uncomplaining *platane* trees, is a spectacle in itself. There are open-air games and shows for children. On at least three of the evenings there are *Grand Bals* with different live 'orchestres', as they say in French. There is dancing by folkloric groups. Traditional Provençal food is served on three evenings: first an *anchoïade*, then an *aïoli*, and on the final evening a *soupe au pistou*. Prior to one of the *Grand Bals*, there is a torchlight procession. Chinese lanterns are handed out to the children. Then, just before the *bal* gets underway, a pine tree is set ablaze. There is, inevitably, a *concours de boules*. Fireworks, too. Yet inextricably linked in and amongst all this are the religious festivities. On 22

July, the actual feast day of the saint, these are centred on the cave as we have seen, with the procession up to it through the forest. But on the following Sunday it is the turn of the basilica to become the focus of a more rumbustious, yet equally valid, day of worship and celebration.

Though there is an Aubade at 7 a.m., it was for the 10.30 Solemn Mass that I planned to drive down from the Hôtellerie. That particular summer was exceptionally hot, the temperature often reaching forty degrees. At 8.30, as I set off to be in time to get a good seat, the temperature was already shooting up. Fanatical cyclists were coming in the opposite direction, straining their way up the hairpin bends. Though of another kind, what devotion!

By 9 a.m. the town was filling up, particularly the medieval streets around the basilica. They had been decked out since the eve of the feast. Cartloads of greenery brought down from the Sainte-Baume foothills now adorned every available lamp-post and balcony. Rosettes in Provençal gold and red added a splash of colour. Stripes in these Catalan colours also feature prominently on the flag, a reminder that Provence was in the possession of the Princes of the House of Barcelona from 1112 to 1245.

On the square in front of the basilica's main entrance, in Provençal dress, groups of men were making music. *Tambourinaires*, they call them. Each fingered a small three-holed pipe – or *galoubet* – in his left hand, while the right hand beat a rhythm on a long, narrow *tambourin*. Other men lined up on either side of the doorway, sporting muskets which they periodically fired into the air *en masse* in a centuries-old expression of joy which northern Europeans now seem to associate only with Middle Eastern countries. The noise was deafening, but circles of women danced on unperturbed. The men wore black, wide-brimmed hats. The women, on the other hand, kept their headgear strapped to their backs. These were vast straw sun-blockers some two feet in diameter.

Inside the basilica, the air was cool; there was still a choice of seats at the front. The bells had begun to peal and would do so incessantly until the service started some forty-five minutes later. Here and there around the sanctuary were sheaves of corn. Provençal flags adorned every conceivable pillar and post, as in the streets. From high up in the vaults were hung slender silk banners in white and mauve – symbols of Mary Magdalen's Paschal joy as well as her repentance. I estimated that – short of driving the latest model of fire engine into the building – no ladder could ever reach these places, so I finally decided to waylay one of the women wearing traditional dress. Since she was placing leaflets on every seat, I assumed she would know enough to be able to satisfy my curiosity. It seems that you have to clamber up onto the roof and then crawl about to specific places where small holes exist for this purpose. Through these a long wire is dropped, to which the banners are attached and the whole thing hauled up high again.

I picked up my leaflet and saw that it contained a litany to Mary Magdalen, as well as hymns and chants in her honour, in Provençal. Here is one typical refrain:

Ounour à Santo Madaleno
Patrouno de Sant Meissemin,

De sei vertu la terro es pleno:
Canten sa glori sènso fin.

Pipes, drums and gunshot resounded all the while. As the time for the service approached, servers, acolytes and an assortment of clergy – among whom were the four friars from the grotto, plus a bishop – processed to the main altar. To my delight, they were followed by a contingent of musicians and musketeers. The shrill soprano of the pipes grew unimaginably louder and more piercing as the players moved up the aisle. The boom of the tambours bounced off the pillars. As for the rifles, however, my childlike hopes were disappointed: these are not fired inside the building, but simply carried. Several of the women, who were now joined by young girls wearing the same traditional dress, carried wicker baskets. The entire party entered the area of the sanctuary, where special seats had been reserved for them, flanking the clergy.

In many southern Catholic countries, after the Consecration, bells are normally tolled. Not the hand-held mini-gadgets of northern climes that are tinkled by some altar server; but loud steeple bells set a-pealing by hefty yanking on ropes. On this occasion however, taking me completely by surprise, it was the pipers and drummers who let rip again.

The significance of the wicker baskets became clear towards the end of the service, when the young girls picked them up again from near the altar and dispersed around the building to distribute hunks of bread. This was *pain bénit* – blessed but not consecrated. Shared with all present, whether or not they have received Holy Communion, it is a symbol of charity and spiritual unity. It is an ancient custom and perhaps a relic of the *agape*, the non-eucharistic common religious meal of the first Christians. Reasonably common in France until recent decades, it survives here and there, at least on special occasions. An equivalent custom in Eastern Orthodox communities, where the bread is called the *antidoron*, is still very much alive.

After Mass on the square in front of the basilica, food and wine were offered by the Municipalité. More dancing took place accompanied by what seemed a never-ending series of salvoes. Small boys darted about among the legs of the men, retrieving the spent cartridges. Other traditionally clad women were selling the latest issue of the Bulletin of the *Association Santo Madaleno*.

Since I intended to stay in town in order to attend the afternoon service and participate in the procession with the relics, I eventually pushed through the crowds to a pavement café. As I took my seat, I noticed that a passing tourist coach was owned, so its advert said, by a firm based in Nice called *Les Phocéens*. It was an unexpected but engaging reminder of those Phocaeans who had originally founded Marseilles and its satellites along the coast.

The café itself – on the Place Malherbe, the main square – adjoins an inn. A sign reminds you that it was here that Lucien Bonaparte (the Emperor's brother) found his bride. On 14 May 1794, he married Christine Boyer, daughter of the innkeeper. Lucien was an interesting character. Stationed during the Revolution as quartermaster in Saint-Maximin, which had been renamed Marathon, he was a leading activist in the local Jacobin club. Yet it was he, nonetheless, who preserved the basilica from the destructive impulses of the notorious Paul Barras. Barras, who was himself born in the Var, represented the region in the revolutionary National Convention. He later became a member of the *Directoire* and was reputedly more ruthless than Robespierre, in whose downfall he had a hand.

The basilica had already been pillaged and ransacked by local revolutionaries, yet it was now threatened with demolition. Lucien invited Barras to come and inspect the building, having first taken care to commandeer the place as a warehouse and to place a deceptive notice over the main door. *Fournitures militaires* it proclaimed. In actual fact, all that the twenty-one side chapels housed were straw, hay, dried vegetables and flour. (I had thought of this episode while waiting for the morning Solemn Mass to begin, after noticing the sheaves of corn in the sanctuary. However, these undoubtedly had more to do with harvest time.)

Barras had already made it clear that in his opinion they should at least melt down the pipes of the organ. As he and the rest of his party approached the main door, they were delighted and surprised to be greeted with the then relatively new revolutionary hymn: the Marseillaise. This had hastily been learned for the occasion by the organist, according to Lucien's instructions. The instrument – a classic of French organ construction by the lay Dominican brother Jean-Esprit Isnard – had been installed a mere twenty years earlier. Benefiting from its four manuals, its forty-three stops, seventy ranks, 2962 pipes, the rendition of the Marseillaise must have been impressive, even to the barbarians of the Revolution, for the day was saved. Barras turned his attention elsewhere.

I reflected on the irony of all this as the resident organist demonstrated the instrument's majesty. It is well known throughout France, regular professional recitals being given.

The highlight of the afternoon service – excepting the *pardon*, the actual procession with the relics – is always the *Panégyrique*, an elaborate and lengthy eulogy on some aspect of Mary Magdalen's life or message.

Sacristans and clergy were busying themselves preparing the processional items, banners and relics. The skull itself in its ornate, golden bust-shaped reliquary had been brought up from the crypt to take pride of place at the entry to the choir stalls. Other early birds were venerating it and lighting candles. As more people poured into the building, the parish priest came out of the sacristy, asking for further volunteers to help carry the portable loudspeaker. Bustling down the aisle he shouted up to the organist: 'Monsieur Bardon, Monsieur Bardon! Don't forget! The *Tantum ergo* a tone higher, if you please!'

Somewhat in the manner of a 'happening', the service did eventually begin. The eulogy was indeed formal and lengthy, but none the worse for that. Each year a different noted Dominican preacher is invited for the occasion. What stays in my mind was the way in which this educated speaker naturally assumed that the three Marys were one and the same. One often reads that this composite Mary Magdalen was definitively dismantled in the wake of Vatican II. In fact, no binding ruling has been taken on the matter. Certainly, here in Provence – as in most places – on the ground, things continue as before.

Reminding us that we were there in this basilica solely because of Mary Magdalen and her message, the eulogist referred to the fact that after all these centuries the front of the building was unfinished, jagged bricks still protruding. Why bother to complete it, he suggested? Surely it was a symbol of Mary herself. The former courtesan no longer desired make-up, required no façade. He pointed to her skull that was placed there before us. A striking contrast, he added – in a comparison that clearly identified Mary with Luke's sinner – to the care this former *femme du monde* must have lavished on her appearance.

Similarly with the ancient litany we were to chant during the procession:

> Saint Mary Magdalen, model of penitence ... *ora pro nobis.*
> You who watered with your tears the feet of Jesus ...
> You who chose the better part ...
> You who obtained the resurrection of your brother, Lazarus ...
> You who, first among the disciples, saw the risen Christ ...
> Apostle of the Apostles ...

No dismantling of a supposedly composite Mary here.

When the time came to assemble for the procession, I noticed that the carriers of the platform on which the skull reliquary rested were not only flanked by relief carriers but also a sizeable collection of musketeers and bearers of halberds and pikestaffs. I guessed – rightly, as it transpired – that these themselves were a 'relic'. A throwback, in fact, to an incident that took place during the self-same procession in 1447. Regarding this, we have the account of Waltheym. This pilgrim from Germany participated in the celebrations some thirty years later, in 1474 – at a time, that is, when eyewitnesses of the incident would still have been alive.

> Early on the Sunday morning we went to the church. The town-crier [...] was announcing peace, blessings and safety to all assembling for such a noble and beneficial feast – except to people from Marseilles. These, he cried, were forbidden from entering the town. It was also forbidden, he announced, to give such people lodging – under pain of death. I asked why this was so and was told that on a certain occasion pilgrims from Marseilles had attended the feast in large numbers and, as the head of Mary Magdalen was being

> carried through the town, they went on the attack, seizing it and running off with it across the fields outside the town walls. Then the citizens of Saint-Maximin gathered together, took up arms, and chased after them. They caught up with them, fought them and successfully recovered the head, bringing it back to the Basilica.

The fear of having the relics stolen, whether during the procession or at other times, was for centuries a feature of local life. Whenever urban development indicated that the city walls and ramparts might be demolished, the decision was postponed. Indeed when they *were* finally pulled down in 1830, they had – surprisingly for an otherwise sleepy country town – twenty square defensive towers.

During my own particular participation in the *pardon*, I fell in, as luck or Providence would have it, with a priest of the Romanian church. It so happened that an elderly Romanian friend, godmother of my children, was at that moment in great need of prayer. So it was easy to strike up a conversation. I was pleased but intrigued, too, by the presence of this Eastern cleric at these celebrations. Just as I had been, on meeting two Orthodox priests from Moscow up at the grotto a few days earlier. Western critics of the Provençal legend all too often turn to the Christian East in their search for ammunition.

Father Faure's reply was similar to that of the Russians. Centuries of prayer, of tenacious adherence to a tradition, of steadfast devotion to a saint, must surely signify something. Our conversation continued as we moved slowly through the narrow streets of the *vieille ville* before bursting out onto the main thoroughfare, bringing the coast-bound traffic to an ignominious halt. I was delighted to learn that his parish was dedicated to St John Cassian. The weekly bulletin for all Romanian parishes in France is itself, he said, called the *Feuillet de Saint Jean Cassien*. He passed me one of his visiting cards and was puzzled as to why I had suddenly started to smile and chuckle. It was the location, I explained. Aix-en-Provence, where I had spent undergraduate time some forty-five years previously, has throughout my life acted as a lodestone.

I raised the question of Cassian's origins, though it was for me a detail of minor importance. As I had guessed, Father Faure was an adherent of the Romanian thesis. His parish had recently offered an icon of the saint to the region of Dobruja, where in this view Cassian is said to have been born. We agreed as to his importance in the spiritual life of the West and, in particular, in this part of Provence, as well as in the local traditions concerning Mary Magdalen.

We parted on yet another coincidental note. I mentioned that Father Henri-Dominique, the senior Dominican *gardien* of the grotto, had invited me to climb with him up to the Saint Pilon chapel on the very summit of the mountain for a Mass in honour of this same saint. As I had already discovered, his feast day, here as in the rest of the Marseilles diocese, is celebrated on 23 July, the day after that of Mary Magdalen.

❧

Reaching the end of my climb that morning, I had paused for breath at the gateway leading to the steep stone steps that take you to the mouth of the cave. Over it is a record of the various monastic orders that have kept watch here: the Dominicans since 1295; before them, from 1079, Benedictines; and, as I read with renewed pleasure, Cassianites from 415 to 1079.

No sooner had I arrived than I was setting off again, on the more strenuous ascent to the summit. There were only a handful of us. Services would be continuing as usual in the cave.

Large black hiking boots protruded now and then, somewhat incongruously, from Henri-Dominique's white robes. I couldn't help noticing the care with which he carried his rucksack. Later, I understood why: it contained a chalice, wine, hosts, and all the other necessary liturgical items. As we approached the minuscule chapel, he brandished a giant iron key which he had dug out from somewhere within the folds of his garments and let us in.

Once inside, it became obvious that the building could hold no more than a dozen people, even squeezed together. A visiting deacon from the Toulouse monastery produced a booklet of harmonized chant, from which three of us sang. As the service got underway, I imagined myself to be back in time, in Maximin's tiny oratory. Father Henri-Dominique's sermon succinctly yet effectively focused on Cassian's spirituality. By the time of the Consecration, we had been joined by a small group of mountaineers, who were overjoyed at this chance discovery.

After the service, as we looked down towards the Mediterranean and La Ciotat in its bay, I recalled that – according to those like Philippe who adhere to the thesis of a Provençal origin for the saint – it was there that he was born and raised. In a recess in the chapel's small porch, someone had left a scallop shell. A *coquille Saint-Jacques* as it is known in French. A reminder that the Sainte Baume had for centuries been on the route of Italian pilgrims bound for Compostella. Indeed, the ancient church in the village of Plan d'Aups, at the western edge of the plateau a few kilometres from the Hôtellerie, is named after St James.

After lunch back at the monastery, I sat chatting with Father Henri-Dominique in the *parloir* that is situated on the outer wall. Admiring the view through the large windows, you have the impression of being in an aeroplane.

'As you know,' he said, 'there are four of us in residence up here again. Just as there were when the Dominicans were first installed at the *Couvent Royal* in town in 1295.'

This was, as it were, the historical reason for their presence here in this remote spot. 'Unusually for us Dominicans,' he added. 'But there's also a ... if you like, a hagiographical reason. You probably know that Mary Magdalen – since 1297, just after we came to Saint-Maximin – has been one of the patron saints of our Order.

Well, certain *fiorettis* ... certain tales ... relate that it is she herself who chooses those who will become members.'

But he had not finished. It was clear that he considered what he was about to say next to be more important still.

'Then there is the missionary reason! At the dawn of this third millennium, when questions of religion seem to be occupying a central place in world affairs, we feel that the Sainte Baume is well placed to emulate Mary in her own missionary role as preacher.'

Preaching is, of course, the special charism of the Order. Every member writes the letters O.P. after his name – Order of Preachers.

'Here you can admire the beauty of a creation that is miraculously preserved. The Gospel message seems concrete and close. You can benefit from the heritage of a living tradition which has marked our culture for centuries.'

Yes, I thought, that was one of the most significant impressions that would stay with me: this tradition was *living*.

Father Henri-Dominique went on to remind me that he and his three colleagues had only taken up residence in 2002. This was after a four-year period of closure, occasioned this time not by hostile human forces but a natural disaster.

It had occurred towards the end of Philippe's tenure. One morning as he went to open the entrance doors of the cave, a massive chunk of the overhanging rock face fell, narrowly missing him. Serious damage was caused. Since the site receives some 500,000 visitors a year, responsible action had to be undertaken. As part of the repair and modernization, a computerized device was installed. This allows for periodic readings to take place which monitor any rock movement, so that potential danger can be averted in advance.

Changing the subject, I expressed my pleasure that John Cassian – at least in this part of western Europe – was receiving his rightful due.

Henri-Dominique smiled. 'In Marseilles we even have a Teacher Training College named after him.'

Philippe, I knew, had devoted one of his booklets to Cassian; but I now learned that Henri-Dominique himself was preparing a talk on Cassian's spirituality, as part of the fortnightly series the Dominicans give on Sunday afternoons throughout the year – alternately here at the cave or down at the Hôtellerie. These cover various aspects of theology, or the sacraments. Or simpler catechism for the young or the curious, for engaged or newly married couples, and so on. In addition to these talks and courses, the daily cycle of monastic offices continues as normal up at the cave, with the permanent availability of a confessor. There are monthly retreats, too. All in all, in the few years since the reopening, an impressive sequence of activities has taken root.

Then there are the grander feast days. In addition to the five days devoted to Mary Magdalen and, of course, Holy Week leading up to Easter, there is Corpus Christi and St Dominic's feast (8 August). But it is for Pentecost and Christmas that a medieval pilgrim's stamina is required. At 10.30 p.m. on Christmas Eve a torchlight procession makes its way up from the Hôtellerie to the cave for Midnight Mass, followed by chocolate and mulled wine at about 2 a.m. Although the temperature inside is constant, outside it can be cruel at that time of year. The Dawn Mass at 8 a.m. up at the Saint Pilon chapel must surely necessitate a very early start and cautious progress, especially if snow is on the ground. For, as I had seen, the going is rough and tricky even at the height of summer.

If the Nativity festivities are for the hardy, it is the Pentecost Pilgrimage that is for the sturdy. For on that Sunday some pilgrims begin a two-day walk all the way from the basilica in town to the grotto, joining up with others at the Hôtellerie on the Monday. Some twenty-five kilometres uphill all the way. To their credit, the friars do not ask pilgrims to undertake any physical exertion they are not prepared to participate in themselves.

Stopping at the fountain, as I walked back down to the plateau, I splashed the cold water over my face and head, and sat for a while on the rim.

❧

It is my last evening at the Hôtellerie in this hot summer. I shall be sorry to leave its genteel dilapidation. Its large octagonal floor tiles. The way its staircases, with their generously wide steps, rise gently and expansively in a spacious mid-nineteenth-century manner. Its sparse, basic yet functional furniture and fittings. All of it honest wood. The simple communal meals at which one so naturally made 'com-panions', sharers of bread.

A fresh sprig of dried lavender and corn has been placed on the table beside a small icon. It depicts the meeting by the tomb between Mary Magdalen and the risen Christ. Is there one like it in every room, I wonder? The Écomusée and the café-bar are closed; the day visitors and hikers gone home. From my room in a quiet wing at the back of the building I can see, in the late luminous light, the cliff face and the monastery buildings. My windows are thrown wide open. The dry air seems to vibrate with heat, even at this hour. The silence is so complete you are compelled to listen to it. The smell of the dried grass in the surrounding plain is impossibly sweet. Without question, this plain, this forest, this grotto are still today places of purification – just as they have been for millennia. For pilgrims down the ages, for the first local Christians, for the Romans, the Greeks, the Celts and the Ligurians. Perhaps, though, the modern pilgrim is more appreciative than were his ancestors of the quality of the air, of the way time can seem suspended. And of the beneficial effect this can have, not just on his senses, but his spirit.

In the stillness, my thoughts and impressions begin to sort themselves out, as when the active waters in a pond begin to settle. Mary Magdalen in Provence? Have I reached any sort of conclusion? Certainly, I am left with the feeling that the Provençal tradition is much older than historians are generally prepared to admit. The coffin ... the cave ... I was becoming convinced that, historically, the coffin was the main thing. The tradition of its being her actual tomb was, I now knew, quite feasible. Yet from a spiritual point of view, it is difficult for the pilgrim to deny the importance of the cave.

As for critics of the legend, I recalled the way Philippe had made me smile with his reference to a quasi-medieval resurgence of Argument from Authority. The sceptics' own chosen authorities, of course. Yet, as I had discovered, it is far from certain that the 710 document found in the sarcophagus at Saint-Maximin has been proved to be a forgery. Nor have the origins of the cult ever been explained away.

❦

As I moved towards the table, looking for a certain notebook, my glance fell again on the icon. In the background, the darkness of the mouth of the cave in which Christ had been laid suddenly caught my attention. Until then I had not fully realized the link between it and the cave here in Provence. A cave where this same woman – this Apostle of the Resurrection, the first human to announce it – is said to have ended her days. If she did come here, did it remind her of that other cave and the joy of that first Easter morning? She will certainly rejoice in the fact that the stress at Saint-Maximin and at the Sainte-Baume is once again – as it usually has been, despite temporary deviations – on the *positive* message of the Gospels.

I have never found Renaissance and post-Renaissance religious art to my taste. Indeed, it is usually theologically suspect. However talented as artists, the painters are able to give free reign to their personal emotions and imaginations – a spiritually dangerous course. Iconographers, on the other hand, traditionally work within a discipline and within a context of prayer and asceticism. Surely, I reflected, much of the misunderstanding surrounding Mary Magdalen and the Provençal tradition can be laid at the door of those western paintings. I was glad to have steered clear of them, as well as of any socio-cultural considerations, during the course of my investigations.

Icons are not naturalistic, not realistic; but are no less truthful for that. In the West, their lack of use of perspective caused them for long to be considered childlike, primitive. So it has been with the Mary Magdalen legend. Perhaps after all, it too – at least the *vie primitive* – is an icon. A stylized, yet eminently theological, verbal icon. More profoundly true than any surface 'naturalism' or so-called 'realism' ever could be.

Below my window is the chapel roof. Behind it rise several cedars of Lebanon. Just out of sight, in their shade, looking up towards the cave, are the tombs of its former *gardiens* – among them Marie-Etienne Vayssière. Philippe's 100-page booklet devoted to his life and work is one of his most attractive publications. Père Vayssière has so profoundly left his mark on the Sainte-Baume that it is difficult to speak of it without referring to him.

As Father Henri-Dominique had remarked, Dominicans – given the *raison d'être* of their foundation – have traditionally been more at home in towns and cities, where the Order of Preachers more easily finds an audience. Volunteers for the post of *gardien* of the grotto have thus tended to be few. This was particularly so in 1900 when Père Vayssière first arrived, as a temporary stopgap. In those days there was, of course, no electricity, no telephone, no radio and no heating other than that provided by the wood that could be gathered in the forest. Politically, with the coming to power of the aggressively anti-clerical Third Republic, things were just as difficult. In 1903 a law banishing religious orders came into force. The *Couvent Royal* in Saint-Maximin – along with the Hôtellerie – was once again forcibly vacated.

Yet Père Vayssière managed to stay on at the grotto by removing his white Dominican habit and adopting the dress of a secular priest. He had new visiting cards printed on which he styled himself simply as *Abbé J. M. Etienne Vayssière, gardien de la Sainte Baume*. Any external sign, any obvious reference to the Dominican Order had to be eliminated.

Since arriving at the grotto in 1900, he had got into the habit of walking down to the Hôtellerie every day – to meet his fellow Dominicans, to exchange a few words with passing pilgrims and perhaps to learn something about the external world. Now that the place had been closed down, he nonetheless continued the habit, chatting instead with local farmers. Before long, however, things were to change. On a certain afternoon, as he approached one of the sixteenth-century oratories near the first fork in the downward path – the so-called '*Quatre chemins*' – he heard, as it were, a rebuking voice: 'Where are you off to? For a spot of distraction? Well, you shall not go!'

There was nothing for it but to turn round and retrace his steps back up to his eyrie. It was at that moment that his 'Magdalenian vocation' was truly born, as *gardien* in more senses than one. From then on, too, he began all at once to recover from the cerebral asthenia that had dogged him for years and bothered his superiors. Steadily he began to grow into the quiet, joyous, saintly figure described by so many acquaintances.

In 1905 – with the passing of the Law of Separation (of Church and State) – even French secular, parish priests came under suspicion and attack. A year later civil servants made their way up to the grotto to effect an inventory of the sort that was despoiling places of worship throughout the land. Vayssière had earlier taken care to place the few relics that had survived earlier acts of depredation – a piece of tibia and some hairs – in the care of a trustworthy family. It was a move that had been repeated down the ages and one which gives further plausibility to the claim that, down at Saint-Maximin, Mary's body was indeed hidden in the eighth century out of fear of a Saracen invasion. Against the odds, he managed to remain in post until, after the armistice of 1918, religious orders were allowed back into France. All in all, this temporary *gardien* remained for thirty-two years.

I took out of my bag Philippe's book about him. There was a passage somewhere in it that had hovered at the back of my mind as I had walked down from my meeting with Father Henri-Dominique.

Towards the end of his life, Father Vayssière had acquired an inner freedom that was not always understood. Yet the passage in question, with whose sentiment I felt sure Father Henri-Dominique would agree, suggested to me that he spoke with the authentic voice of Tradition.

> What is an apostle? Someone who simply preaches, coming and going, bustling about, busying himself with the care of souls? No doubt all this is necessary, but it isn't the heart of the matter. It's just the outer peel, the surface ... It is possible to exert oneself to a considerable extent, leading a life that is externally very active, and yet be a mediocre apostle. Or not even an apostle at all... While, on the other hand, nothing could be more authentically apostolic than a soul that is withdrawn, silent and to all appearances inactive...

Had he known it, he would have agreed with the seemingly paradoxical counsel of St Seraphim of Sarov: 'Acquire inner peace and thousands around you will be saved'. It is no accident that people have detected a spiritual kinship between Father Vayssière and Charles de Foucauld, the Saharan hermit whom he welcomed here on three occasions, turning points in Charles' life. He would surely smile to see that, as the 22 July procession reaches the entrance to the cave on its final station before entering, the prayer that is recited is Charles' own: 'May this dear Saint Mary Magdalen teach us Love ...' It is what he himself had always stressed. Emphasis on the aspects of penance, understood negatively – a misreading of the tradition, as I have tried to show – annoyed him. 'She is the saint of Love,' he would insist. 'It wasn't her penitence that Jesus praised, but her love. "She loved much," he said.'

Love. It is the fulfilment of the Law, says Paul in Romans. It is the new commandment given by Christ at the Last Supper. It is the only definition of God contained in the New Testament.

As is well documented, Père Vayssière had the gift of insight, of spiritual discernment. People felt that what he said to them went straight to their hearts and corresponded exactly to what, deep down, they were at that moment in need of hearing. In this he seems, appropriately enough, to have been rather like the old Desert Fathers whose method and wisdom John Cassian had so long ago wished to introduce into this part of France.

Yet he was not particularly forthcoming about the controversies surrounding the tradition, preferring to maintain a discreet silence. His one reply, when pestered for his opinion, is more telling in its deceptive simplicity than any product of intellectual scholarship or document-obsessed research. It can serve as our concluding remark.

'Mary Magdalen? I don't know whether she came or whether she didn't. What I know is that she is here!'

Appendix*

Arguments in favour of believing that the unnamed sinner in Luke 7 is the same woman as Mary, sister of Martha and Lazarus.

In a sense, all depends on two short verses in John's Gospel: 'Now a certain man was ill, Lazarus of Bethany, the village of Mary and her sister Martha. *It was that Mary who anointed the Lord with ointment and wiped his feet with her hair whose brother Lazarus was ill*' (11:1–2). To which anointing is John referring? An event in the past, the one recorded by Luke in Chapter 7? Or the occasion at Bethany which John is himself about to describe in his next chapter (12:1–8)? It is fashionable today to opt for the latter view. Yet, as Bruckberger insisted, this interpretation flies in the face both of grammatical sense and of the rudiments of rhetoric.

As for grammatical sense, no such tense errors – the use of an aorist participle to indicate a future event – can be found in the rest of John's Gospel. In fact, the Greek participles in question might more accurately be translated as '*had* anointed' and '*had* wiped' making the past reference even clearer. Moreover, when John does wish to refer to a future event, he shows himself quite capable of doing so.

Undeterred, some critics have pointed out that, by the

* For many of the following ideas, I am indebted to Bruckberger and Feuillet.

time the Gospels came to be written, the anointing described in Luke 7 was a past event. This, they claim, is what explains John's use of the aorist in 11:2.

However, many examples can be cited to throw doubt on this line of reasoning. Here is one from the same chapter: '[Caiphas] prophesied that Jesus should die [in Greek = *was to die*] for the nation' (v.51). This prophecy too is for both writer and reader a past event; so why does John adhere to the use of a future construction? Simply because, as throughout his Gospel, his temporal perspective or backcloth is that of the unfolding ministry of Jesus: what is past at a particular point in the narrative is past; what is to come is to come. One further example will help to make this clearer. It is to be found a mere page away from the verse that concerns us, in the very passage that describes the Bethany anointing. '... Judas Iscariot, one of his disciples (he *who was to betray* him)' (12:4). John's sensitivity to tenses is made all the clearer when we compare this with the equivalents in Matthew and Mark. There, we find that Judas is described more simply as 'he who betrayed him'. In his very next chapter, John goes on to describe this betrayal in detail. Thus, if our key verse (11:2) likewise refers to an incident about to be described in a following chapter, why does John not use, here too, the selfsame construction?

Every other verse in John that has some grammatical similarity with 11:2 likewise refers to a past incident. For example: 'Nicodemus, *he that had gone* to him before ...' (7:50).

Perhaps the most telling example is the following – again found a mere page away, in the passage describing the Bethany anointing. Translated fairly literally so as to capture John's original, it reads as follows: 'Six days before the Passover, Jesus came to Bethany where Lazarus was, *the one who had died*, whom he raised from the dead' (12:1).

It seems to be a habit of John's to introduce a parenthesis in this way, in order to identify a person in relation to a past event that is already known about. Admittedly, if 11:2 does refer back to Luke 7, it would be the only case where the past action is not also related by John himself. Yet it is an accepted fact that John was familiar with the other Gospels and took it for granted that his readers were, too. Probably for this reason, he often mentions briefly and, as it were, *en passant* events that were far more important than the anointing described by Luke. So it is with the baptism of Jesus (1:32), the imprisonment of John the Baptist (3:24), the appointment of the Twelve (6:67), and Barabbas (18:40). His particular contribution – as a privileged friend and eyewitness, though writing later than Matthew, Mark and Luke – was to add details or clarify a point of chronology or personality.

Some have conveniently suggested that the key phrase in John 11:2 is a later gloss, regardless of the fact there is no manuscript tradition of such an addition. Yet even if it were a gloss and referred to a past event, it would still show that the first Christians did equate the sister of Lazarus with Luke's unnamed sinner. If, on the other hand, it were a gloss referring to the *future*, it would be nonsensical. Which brings us to the question of logic and rhetoric.

If 11:2 referred to the anointing at Bethany which John is about to describe, it would be a redundant and pointless verse, merely confusing something that would be perfectly clear without it. Why should one insist on making it say the opposite of what it does say?

As for John's account of the anointing at Bethany, it is only when read in conjunction with Luke's earlier anointing that it begins to reveal its full significance. The differences between the two passages paradoxically help establish the connection.

In Luke, the sequence is quite plausible. Jesus was 'reclining' at table (as the Greek states) in the contemporary manner, on a divan with outstretched feet. The meal to which he had been invited would have been semi-public (possibly in a courtyard) and of the ceremonial kind given for visiting rabbis. As Mary approaches Jesus – probably intending to anoint his head, according to customary etiquette, even though she was not the host – she is suddenly overcome by her proximity to his charismatic presence and, pausing by his feet, begins to shed tears. Embarrassed and nonplussed as to how to cope with the situation, she improvises by using her hair. She kisses and dries Jesus' feet and – to compensate, as it were, for her blunder – anoints them. The anointing of the head gets forgotten, the more so as Simon begins to voice his critical comments.

On the occasion of the second anointing, at Bethany, Mary's behaviour is far less natural. What is the point of wiping, not tears – for there are none – but perfumed ointment? Moreover, if any wiping *were* required, why – unnecessarily so on this occasion, since she has no need to improvise – does Mary not hesitate to use her hair again? It seems that every action is a symbolic, repeat gesture.

But what of the discrepancies between the Bethany incident as described by John and the version given by Mark (14:3–9; cf. Matthew 26:6–13)? This is surely the same event at the same place – named as Bethany – and at the same time in Jesus' ministry, the week before the crucifixion. (The fact that John says 'six days before the Passover', whereas Mark has 'two days', poses no real problem, for John is simply referring to Jesus' arrival in Bethany.)

Yet the differences are obvious enough. In Mark the host is named as Simon the Leper (a nickname he had presumably retained after being cured by Jesus). In John no host is specified, though neither is it stated that the supper was held in the house of Lazarus and his sisters. In fact, the implication is perhaps that it was not. For why would John state that Lazarus 'was one of those at table with him'? If the meal had been served in Lazarus' own house, that would have been taken for granted or conveyed by the inclusion of some introductory phrase such as 'at the house of Lazarus'. The fact that, again according to John, 'Martha served' does not mean we must necessarily imagine her to be in her own house, as anyone who has lived in the Middle East can testify. Nor does John mean that she undertook this service single-handedly; merely that she was *among* those who served, that she helped out in an area where she felt 'at home'. Even today, most social functions in the average parish reveal that certain people will naturally always gravitate towards certain tasks. Perhaps Simon had heard that Jesus was in the vicinity, visiting Lazarus and his sisters, and had invited them all to dinner. Finally, is it not relevant to our argument that both John and Luke (in his Chapter 10) single out a 'Martha' as being the one who takes care of the practicalities? Surely it is the same pair of sisters in both Gospels. We must remember not only that John assumed that his readers would be familiar with Luke and the other Gospels but also that in Luke we often find echoes of John. For even though the writing of Luke's Gospel predates that of John, the Johannine tradition itself is older. Moreover, does Luke not say that he had consulted 'those who from the beginning were eyewitnesses and ministers of the word' (1:2)? John was undoubtedly one of these. Indeed, it was possibly from him that Luke obtained his information about Martha and Mary. Certainly, what he says about the two women and their characters (10:38–42) fits perfectly with John's depiction of them in Chapters 11 and 12.

Though Mark names the village as Bethany, he does not identify the woman. Furthermore, he refers only to an anointing of the head, not the feet or any wiping of them. Yet these seeming discrepancies arise only because John, for his part, is generally concerned, as mentioned, to add further details to a story already known. Anointing the head of distinguished guests was relatively common and therefore not particularly unusual. If, then, this were *all* that happened at Bethany, it is difficult to see why Jesus should have praised the woman so highly ('she has done a beautiful thing to me', Mark 14:6) and why he should have made the remarkable prophecy concerning her: 'she has anointed my body beforehand for burying. And truly, I say to you, wherever the gospel is preached in the whole world, what she has done will be told in memory of her' (Mark 14:8–9).

By itself, an anointing of the head would not have

connoted an anticipation of burial. However, an anointing of both head and feet – peformed deliberately this time, rather than accidentally – might be so interpreted. It is reasonable to assume that at Bethany two separate actions (affecting head first, then feet) were performed *successively*. 'From head to toe.' These extremities would, of course, be the only parts of a still living, clothed body that could be anointed in public.

— ❧ —

Supposing Luke's unnamed sinner to be the same person as Mary, sister of Lazarus, can we go further and claim that she is also the same person as Mary Magdalen?

The texts themselves cannot definitively prove these things, one way or the other. Yet, if we examine the convergence of probabilities – a method considered quite respectable by professional historians – we can certainly claim that there is a case to be made.

To begin with, although some have inexplicably denied this, the general character traits of Mary Magdalen do match those of the unnamed sinner and of the Mary we meet at Bethany. There is the same single-minded audaciousness. She doesn't hesitate to step forward at a public banquet given in honour of Jesus. With dogged determination, she goes to the tomb and, finding it empty, asks the supposed gardener whether he has removed her Lord. 'Tell me where you have laid him and I will take him away,' she boldly asserts (John 20:15–16). 'I', she says, not 'we', utterly dismissive and disdainful of any practical complications her words might imply. Does this not remind us of the single-minded Mary who was criticized by her sister Martha for ignoring the practicalities of being a hostess and preferring to sit spellbound at the feet of Jesus (Luke 10:38–42)? The same Mary who was nonetheless praised by Jesus for this. Unlike her sister, who is 'troubled and anxious about many things', she has the instinctive ability to focus on the 'one thing [that] is needful'. Jesus might well have had at the back of his mind the words from Deuternomy with which he had himself earlier countered the Devil's temptation: 'Man does not live by bread alone but by everything that proceeds out of the mouth of the Lord' (8:3). Here – sitting at the Lord's feet in the traditional pose of a disciple, 'listening to his teaching' (v.39), just as she was later to sit fearlessly and doggedly opposite the sepulchre (Matthew 27:61) – was someone who had understood. Indeed, it is surely a further sign of their single identity that the unnamed sinner, Mary the sister of Lazarus, and Mary Magdalen repeatedly show themselves able to understand the message of Jesus more instinctively than anyone else in the Gospels.

We know – from Jesus' final words, his 'new commandment' which sums up all he had done and said – that this central message might be described as the need for unlimited, compassionate love. He washed his uncomprehending disciples' feet as part of his attempts to convey this message. Yet one other person in the Gospels had performed the selfsame action before him: Mary. Not ceremonially, as a social convention; but in a scandalously excessive manner – scandalous whether on account of the profusion of her tears, or the way she 'ceased not to kiss' Jesus' feet (Luke 7:45), or the self-forgetful use of her hair, which so impressed Jesus (v.44) and which should have been covered. Or, indeed, on account of the excessive quantity – a pound at Bethany – and the cost of the perfumed oil used. An excess which Jesus will have welcomed, not as the actions of an emotionally unstable woman but as an image, albeit imperfect, of his own limitless mercy. (In Greek, the words 'oil' and 'mercy' are semantically related.) We are accustomed to talking of the Prodigal Son, prodigal because of the lavishness with which he spent his inheritance. We tend to forget that, in the parable, the central figure is the Prodigal Father, prodigal in pouring out his love. Surely Jesus will have appreciated that, even if on a far humbler level, Mary's actions too were characterized by this same prodigality. Can as much be said, before the Resurrection, of any of the Apostles? To the *maximalism* of his entire teaching corresponds Mary's instinctively maximalist response. It is little wonder he described what she had done to him as 'beautiful'.

The same characteristics, the same spiritual closeness to Jesus can be seen when he comes to Bethany after the death of Lazarus (John 11). To begin with, Mary is unaware that he is coming and has stayed in the house, being consoled. Even though Martha's meeting with Jesus gives rise to his solemn declaration that he is the Resurrection and the Life (v.25) and to Martha's profession of faith, yet still Jesus does nothing about Lazarus. Instead he sends Martha back to the house for Mary. 'The Teacher is here,' she whispers, 'and is calling for you' (v.28). Once more, Mary's single-mindedness shows itself, in the way she instantly snaps out of her immobility, getting up so 'quickly' (v.31) that the Jews who had been consoling her seem to have commented on it. (The Teacher will again call her, by name, and rouse her out of a similar state of grief – in the garden on Easter morning.)

Once Mary has met up with Jesus, she repeats the same comment as her sister – 'Lord, if you had been here, my brother would not have died.' Unlike Martha, she weeps. It is as if Mary is a catalyst, for Jesus' reaction now changes. He is 'deeply moved in spirit and troubled'. 'Where have you laid him?' he asks. It is the very question that Mary will put to the 'gardener' on Easter morning (John 20:15). Mary weeps, and now Jesus joins her: 'Jesus wept' (11:35). Amid this unique converging of emotions, who is it that is concerned with practicalities such as the stink from the festering corpse? Martha, of course (v.39).

Returning to the anointing at Bethany, there is one detail that further encourages us to identify Mary the sister of Lazarus with Mary Magdalen. One of its most striking features, as already mentioned, is that Jesus interprets it as being a prophetic anticipation of his burial. With good reason, for by the end of John's Chapter 11 the Sanhedrin has already decided to put him to death. 'She has anointed my body beforehand for burying,' we read in Mark (14:8).

Similarly, Matthew has, 'In pouring this ointment on my body she has done it to prepare me for burial' (26:12). Strangely, the Vulgate of John's account – and those translations based on it – over-rationalize the statement, as follows: 'Let her alone, *let her keep it* [*ut ... servet*] for the day of my burial' (12.7). However, the best Greek manuscripts, including that used by the Orthodox Church, unequivocally do *not* refer to a future event. 'She *has kept it* for the day of my burial' is the clear meaning of the original.

We should resist the temptation to 'correct' the mistranslation so as to make it imply that Mary should 'keep the *memory*' of what had been performed; or that, having only partly used her supply, she should keep *the rest* for later. Admittedly, John does not explicitly say that the entire contents had been used, but his text does suggest as much. Indeed it is precisely such a prodigality that occasions Judas' criticism. It is very probable that John's text represents Jesus' words faithfully. Certainly Jesus' language, as conveyed by John, often does have this enigmatic character. In other words, prophetically and symbolically, and indeed as the versions of Matthew and Mark suggest, Bethany is the actual *beginning* of Jesus' burial. 'She has kept it for the day of my burial': in sacred time, the dawning of that day has arrived, now, at Bethany.

In John there is no account of the women who went to the tomb with spices. However, in the other three Gospels, it is Mary Magdalen who heads the group of named, intrepid myrrh-bearers. The sister of Lazarus – she who prophesied the burial – disappears from the text during the Passion; Mary Magdalen suddenly reappears. Can we not suppose that they are one and the same? We can at the very least claim that an anointing such as that performed at Bethany would have been, for Mary Magdalen, perfectly in character.

The two women share, of course, the same name: Mary. It is worth reminding ourselves that 'Mary of Bethany' – a convenient appellation much used by critics and writers – is never used by the evangelists themselves.

But 'Mary of Magdala', 'Mary Magdalen' – surely this always refers to a separate identifiable person? Things are not so clear-cut. The evangelists sometimes write 'Mary of Magdala' just as they sometimes write 'Jesus of Nazareth'. At other times they simply write 'Mary', just as they write 'Jesus'. An examination of the various instances suggests that they resort to 'Magdalen' only when the context (e.g. a reference to Bethany, Martha or Lazarus) has not removed all possible ambiguity. For example, in Luke 8:2 and Mark 16:9, the cognomen 'Mary Magdalen' is used in order to clarify which Mary it was who had been plagued by seven demons. Again, when John is describing her solitary approach to the tomb, having first made clear who he is referring to (20:1), he simply calls her Mary (v.11). It is by this, her real name, that the risen Jesus calls her in their moving exchange in the garden (v.16).

Turning to another objection, we must admit that the Mary whom John describes as living at Bethany must also have lived in Galilee, since that is where Magdala is situated and that is where Luke's anointing took place. This woman must therefore have followed Jesus to Jerusalem, from which Bethany is two miles distant. In fact, this seems to be exactly what did happen to Mary Magdalen. We are specifically told by Luke (8:1–3) that she accompanied Jesus as he went 'through cities and villages' and 'provided for' him and the Twelve Apostles 'out of [her] means'. Furthermore, there are several references in the closing chapters of the Gospels specifically indicating that she, Joanna and other women had followed Jesus from Galilee to Jerusalem (e.g. Luke 23:49, 55; 24:10).

She might, of course, have belonged to a family that – like many wealthy people then as now – had two houses, one in or near the capital, the other elsewhere. Since there is a strong tradition that Mary was of an aristocratic Sadduceean household, this is entirely feasible. Even if we reject this particular classification of her family, there is enough evidence in the Gospels – the purchase, for example, of a large quantity of extremely expensive nard – to show that she certainly did have considerable independent means.

Luke, in his account of the household of Martha and Mary (Ch. 10), is tantalizingly vague as to its whereabouts. Ultimately, this does not pose a major problem. Jesus has apparently left Galilee but is still far from Jerusalem. Yet we need not suppose that there is a third house! Luke's Chapter 10 comes at the beginning of his long central section which continues until what we now call Palm Sunday and in which he includes many episodes that he does not locate precisely. The whole is cast in the form of a journey. Not an actual journey which can be plotted, but a symbolic one. Nonetheless, it is interesting that his account of Jesus entering the house of Martha and Mary is immediately preceded by the parable of the Good Samaritan with its reference to the road from Jericho to Jerusalem, the very road that Jesus was taking, the road on which Bethany is situated.

— ❧ —

If there was indeed only one woman, in what sense was Mary Magdalen a sinner? What were her 'seven demons'?

It is significant that Magdala was not far from Tiberias on the western shore of the Sea of Galilee. This was the new capital of Herod Antipas, Tetrach of Galilee, founded around AD 20. During its construction an ancient cemetery was uncovered. As a result, as Josephus records in his *Antiquities of the Jews* (xviii, 2.3), it was repulsive for devout Jews to live there on account of the ritual impurity that would contaminate them. Herod accordingly used compulsion as well as various benefits (such as free housing and land) to entice not only Galileans but all sorts of foreigners to come and live there. The fact that it was a Gentile city with Hellenistic architecture, customs and religion also made it suspect in the eyes of strict Jews. The loose morals of Herod and his court – of which his birthday banquet complete with dancing girls gives us a brief taste – would have been anathema.

Of all the evangelists, it is not surprising that it is the Greek convert Luke, writing primarily for Gentiles, who seems most interested in Herod's court. Much of his information may well have come from Manaen, one of the leaders in the Church at Antioch, traditionally believed to have been Luke's home town. Interestingly, in Acts (13:1) Luke informs us that this Manaen 'had been brought up with Herod the tetrarch'. (Some translations describe him as 'a member of Herod's court', or 'Herod's foster brother'.)

What is undeniable is that Luke's brief reference to 'Joanna, wife of Chuza, Herod's steward' (8:3) is more revealing than its brevity might suggest. It gives us an intriguing glimpse, but a far from fanciful one, of what Mary Magdalen's background might well have been. To begin with, it follows immediately on from the verse in which she is first named. The two women are obviously close companions, as is made even clearer by the fact that they are still inseparable at the end of the Gospel (24:10). As for the job of steward, we should not underestimate the importance of Chuza's position. We might call to mind the office of Lord High Steward in our own country, the very first of the nine Great Offices of State – more senior than the position of Lord High Chancellor or Lord High Treasurer. Whatever Chuza's precise functions at Herod's court, he was clearly high up in the pecking order as, by implication, was his wife.

Nevertheless, whenever Luke names Jesus' female helpers and followers, it is Mary Magdalen who comes first, as she always does in all four Gospels – except in John's list of women who stood at the foot of the Cross, where Mary, the mother of Jesus, and her sister naturally take precedence (John 19:25). Yet, returning to Luke's list, the fact that Mary precedes even Joanna in itself suggests that she was a person of some importance. How did she come to know Joanna? Perhaps she was herself a member of Herod's court. Her presence there would help to explain several things in the Gospels, especially that of Luke.

It might, for example, help us understand how Mary (and

Joanna) came to hear about Jesus and perhaps how she came into contact with him, directly or otherwise. (In Matthew 15:39 we read that on one occasion Jesus sailed to the coasts of Magdala, but little can be read into this.)

Of all the evangelists, it is Luke who is not only the great stylist, but also the great craftsman. Does he not state at the beginning that it is his express intention, 'having followed all things closely for some time, to write an *orderly* account' (1:3)? This surely implies a concern for psychological as well as logical, if not strictly chronological, development. With this in mind, Bruckberger's suggestion that the incident of the unnamed sinner is set within a specific framework is particularly attractive.

Chapter 7 opens with the healing of the Gentile centurion's servant at Capernaum. 'Not even in Israel have I found such faith,' remarks Jesus (v.9) in a phrase which foreshadows his commendation of the unnamed sinner's faith. Next comes the raising to life of the widow of Nain's son. Both miracles are evidence for John that Jesus is indeed the Messiah. The Pharisees and lawyers, however, are unimpressed at this 'friend of tax collectors and sinners' (v.34). Yet, concludes Jesus, 'wisdom is justified by all her children' (v.35). It is immediately after this comment that there begins the account of the anointing by the unnamed sinner. Thus, though often skipped over, it is a comment which not only sums up the preceding section, which highlighted John the Baptist, but which also refers forward to the unnamed sinner. But what does it mean? Moreover, does it give us a further clue as to the identity of this sinner?

It is generally accepted that Luke spent much time in the company of Paul, even being his travelling companion, as can be seen from Acts. Bruckberger reminds us of this when he claims to detect a parallel to Luke's structuring of these passages in the following verses from Paul's First Letter to the Corinthians: 'Jews look for signs and Greeks seek after wisdom; but we preach Christ crucified, unto Jews a stumbling block, and unto Gentiles foolishness; but unto them that are called, both Jews and Greeks, Christ the power of God, and the wisdom of God' (1:22–4). Is Luke giving us a fleshed out example of this? John the Baptist and disciples would thus represent the 'Jews looking for signs'. (Of which Jesus proceeds to give them examples, adding – using the same image as Paul, though it is too often paraphrased – 'blessed is he who shall find no occasion of *stumbling* in me', v.23.) A Hellenized Mary Magdalen, on the other hand, would represent devotees of Greek wisdom, such as was lauded at Herod's court. In other words, she plays the same role in the Greek quest for wisdom as John played in the prophetical tradition of Israel.

All in all, it seems perfectly reasonable to suggest that Luke is indeed hinting at an association between John and Mary. John the Baptist certainly did cause a stir at court with his outspoken criticism of Herod's marriage to Herodias, and it is possible that it was he who provided the link. Had Mary and Joanna had a change of heart? Possibly after John's gruesome martyrdom. Perhaps Herodias or her daughter (traditionally known as Salome, from Josephus' account) had been a friend of theirs. Perhaps they had been present at the banquet given by Herod at which the request for John's head had been made. It seems reasonable to assume that Joanna – or, at the very least, her husband – had attended.

Without doubt, news of Jesus was circulating at Herod's court, for Luke tells us that his curiosity had been aroused when 'he heard of all that was done', and that 'he sought to see him' (Luke 9:7–9). Included in what was being done was the change wrought, for example, in several women, among whom we find named Mary Magdalen and Joanna.

If the activities of Jesus or his disciples had indeed caused such prominent members of Herod's court as Mary and Joanna to change their ways and turn their backs on his corrupt court, we can well imagine why it is not long before Jesus is warned (in a verse found only in Luke), 'Herod wants to kill you' (13:31). Luke is also the only evangelist to tell us of Jesus' silent appearance before Herod, who mocks him before sending him back to Pilate, thus sealing his fate (23:8–12).

❦

However, if the sinful woman is indeed Mary Magdalen, why does Luke not name her? After all, as his text makes clear, she was well known to Simon and his friends, at least by sight. It is unlikely that such an unusual incident will quickly have been forgotten. As someone who prided himself on having thoroughly researched his information, Luke could surely have made enquiries.

We can only anwer by pointing to his general habit of toning down or omitting material that his readers might find derogatory. Is it for a similar reason that Luke – usually so keen to include his special information on Herod – is silent on the colourful account of Herod's birthday banquet and the events that lead up to John's fate? Perhaps, as already suggested, because he knew that Mary and Joanna had been in some way involved, if only by association.

Luke's treatment of the Apostles is another well-known example of this tendency. Indeed, the way he introduces us to Matthew – another sinner, by virtue of his employment as tax collector – is similar to the instance which concerns us at present. In describing his calling by Jesus, Luke refers to him only as Levi (5:27). When, in the following passage, he lists the names of the disciples, 'Levi' is dropped and replaced by his new name, 'Matthew' (6:15). Those in the know would understand. (In his own Gospel, Matthew is less reticent, but that is his prerogative.)

Perhaps Luke has done the same with the way he introduces us to Mary Magdalen. The account of the unnamed sinner seems deliberately to be sandwiched between the reference to 'children of wisdom' and the explicit naming of Mary, as someone who had needed to be healed – at the very start of what we now call the next chapter. (These divisions are merely a thirteenth-century editorial device.)

Assuming her to be the unnamed sinner, Mary's probable connection with Herod's court and its Hellenism might also help explain the nature of her sin. It is clear that the anointing described by Luke does not represent her first contact with Jesus. She comes prepared. Something has already happened. In some way her heart has already been touched. We know – since Luke tells us at the beginning of the chapter – that Jesus has recently been preaching and healing along the western shore of the Sea of Galilee, specifically in Capernaum, a town quite close to both Magdala and Tiberias. Perhaps Mary had been among the crowd.

Those who would draw a false contrast between Luke's unnamed sinner and Mary at Bethany – the former displaying feelings of remorse, the latter veneration, gratitude and love – are guilty of misinterpreting the former's tears. For everything she does betrays nothing if not gratitude and veneration. Nor can true remorse for sin exist without love – love for the persons injured, who are ultimately Jesus and his Father.

Luke's Greek text describes her as 'a woman in the city who was a sinner'. The word for prostitute is not used here. Perhaps she had simply been following the Greek ideal of the 'free woman', and had been a courtesan in Herod's 'city', then as since a respected high-class, cultured calling in the eyes of some. Whether or not she was a courtesan, even being associated with Herod's court would, as mentioned, have classified her as 'a sinner', someone ritually unclean.

This would not have bothered Jesus. But what are we to make of the 'seven demons' that he cast out of her (Luke 8:2; Mark 16:9)? This must surely imply something more than ritual uncleanness.

We must first remember that in the New Testament the word 'demon' rarely refers to 'possession' in the strong sense. Indeed, Jesus and John the Baptist were themselves more than once accused of 'having a demon'. Rather, it is usually a synonym for an 'unclean' or 'evil spirit'. This is why, in one verse, Luke can quite naturally roll the three terms together, writing of the 'spirit of an unclean demon' (4:33). It may even simply refer to a speech impediment, as in Luke 11:14, where we read of 'a demon that was dumb'. In fact, this is the way it is most often used; namely, in conjunction with references to diseases or infirmities. (A syntactical conjunction which points to a deeper link.) Moreover, this is precisely how it is used in the very verse which precedes Luke's reference to Mary's seven demons. In it she is described, far less dramatically, as being one of a group who had been 'healed of evil spirits and infirmities' (Luke 8:2).

The number seven, of course, is simply a Hebrew idiom indicating plentifulness or abundance, as Luke's account of Jesus' teaching on forgiveness makes clear: 'and if [your brother] sins against you seven times in the day, and turns to you seven times, and says "I repent", you must forgive him' (17:4). Later in his Gospel (11:24–6), Luke relates some general teaching of Jesus on demons in which he again uses the number seven as an intensifier. 'Then [the unclean spirit] goes and brings seven other spirits more evil than himself and they enter and dwell there; and the last state of that man becomes worse than the first.' Interestingly, it is an idiom which seems to reinforce the identity of Mary Magdalen (and her many demons) with Luke's unnamed sinner, and 'her many sins' (7:47). If she *had* led the life of a courtesan at a Gentile court, this would have meant that she was indeed guilty of gross (hence the number seven) sexual uncleanness or impurity.

Curiously, several critics and some early Church Fathers (mostly Greek) – have been embarrassed by the suggestion that Mary the sister of Lazarus (whether or not she was the same person as Mary Magdalen) might be Luke's 'sinful woman', whose sins they definitely assume to have been sexual in nature. How could such a public sinner, they argue, be a preferred friend of Christ?

The revered John Chrysostom is typical. In his *Homily LXII* on John Chapter 11, he sharply differentiates the 'grave and earnest' Mary of Bethany from Luke's unnamed sinner, whom he unequivocally brands a harlot (πόρνη). His view has come to be normative in the Greek Church. Luke's sinner is, for example, systematically and automatically styled a harlot in the Prayers Before Communion.

It is easy to see how the above attitude might deter some from thinking of Luke's sinner and Mary the sister of Lazarus as being one and the same, and how it has come to reinforce the Greek view that they were separate women. Yet it is a line of reasoning that runs counter to the teaching of Jesus. St Augustine, on the other hand – having been a great sinner himself – was free from such embarrassment. Some argue that, in his *Homilies on the Gospel of John* (written *c.* 416), he seems to leave the Identity question in doubt, pointing to the following words in italics:

> Now the sister of Lazarus (*if indeed it was she* who anointed the feet of the Lord with perfumed oils and wiped his feet with her hair after bathing them with tears) was raised from the dead more truly than her brother; she was freed from the weight of her bad habits. She was indeed a celebrated sinful woman. It is of her that has been said: 'Many sins have been forgiven her because she has loved much.' (XLIX Ch.xi)

Yet the entire thrust of the paragraph, as Feuillet points out, leaves no doubt that he does identify Mary of Bethany with Luke's sinner. He also recognizes that, as we have said, no definitive proof can be provided by the texts alone. The conditional clause is there to make clear that this is his personal opinion. He has no wish to impose it, especially in a homily.

That this is, nevertheless, his considered view is clear from his more academic work of exegesis, *The Harmony of the Gospels* (II.79), in which – despite the acknowledged problems – he is happy to believe that John 11 refers back to Luke 7: 'But my theory is that it was the same Mary who did this deed on two separate occasions, the one being that which Luke has put on record.' This is an earlier work (*c.* 400), but there is no need to assume that the conditional clause in the *Homilies*, written some sixteen years later, indicates that he is beginning to change his mind.

Moreover, in his final years Augustine wrote two books of *Retractations* in which he revises, explains and corrects his life's work. He does *not* change or correct his views concerning the matter under discussion. They have been constant. Ambrose and Jerome, like so many other Fathers, had vacillated in their opinion; it was Augustine who established and settled the western tradition.

Ironically, despite John Chrysostom's opinion and influence, the service books of the Orthodox Church – considered to be normative – do after all equate Luke's sinner (styled a 'harlot') with the woman who anointed Jesus at Bethany (as related by Matthew, Mark and John). This is made repeatedly clear, as seen earlier, by the texts for Great (Holy) Wednesday.

We need, then, have no puritanical qualms about assuming that Mary of Bethany and Luke's sinner might be the same person (and the same person as Mary Magdalen), even if her sins were sexual in nature. Even if she had been a courtesan, a high-class harlot. Did Jesus not rebuke his self-righteous opponents with the comment that it was precisely 'tax collectors and harlots' who were entering the kingdom of God before them, because they had listened to John the Baptist's call for repentance?

Interestingly, it is a verse that appears only in the Gospel of tax collector Matthew (21:31). If he himself was an example of the one group, surely we need not worry about seeing Mary Magdalen as a prime example of the other. We are familiar with the parable of The Tax Collector and the Pharisee, recorded by Luke in Chapter 18; yet there is a sense in which the anointing described in his Chapter 7 might itself be described as an incident which Jesus transformed into being an 'acted' parable: The Harlot and the Pharisee.

❦

The identification of Mary Magdalen as a reformed courtesan, far from being an objectionable error, points to one of the Bible's most persistent themes. As Benedicta Ward puts it, in her book *Harlots of the Desert*, '[she] takes to herself the image of unfaithful Israel, so graphically described by the prophets as a prostitute in relation to God. [. . .] It is in this profoundly illuminating sense that Mary of Magdala assumes the character of a prostitute, not because lust is a specially terrible sin but because she is all sinners in so far as all sin is unfaithfulness to the covenant of love'. One could go further and claim that this pivotal role of hers in the Gospels – throughout which Jesus is continually castigating 'this adulterous generation' – would be made even more meaningful, if she had been a repentant courtesan factually as well as metaphorically.

Select Bibliography

Albanès, J. H., *Le couvent royal de Saint-Maximin en Provence* (Marseilles, 1880).

André-Vincent, P. I., OP, *La Sainte-Baume* (Paris, 1950).

Augustine of Hippo, *The Harmony of the Gospels*, in *Nicene and Post-Nicene Fathers,* Series 1, vol. 6, edited by P. Schaff (Grand Rapids and Edinburgh, 1886).

Augustine of Hippo, *Homilies on the Gospel of John*, in *Nicene and Post-Nicene Fathers*, Series 1, vol. 7, edited by P. Schaff (Grand Rapids and Edinburgh, 1886).

Augustine of Hippo, *The Retractations*, translated by M. I. Bogan (Washington, DC, 1968).

Beausobre, I. de, *Flame in the Snow* (London, 1945).

Bérenger, J., *Sainte Marie-Madeleine en Provence* (Marseilles, 1925).

Boyer, R., *La chartreuse de Montrieux – au XIIe et XIIIe siècles*, 3 vols (Marseilles, 1980).

Bridonneau, Y., *Le tombeau de Marie-Madeleine* (Aix-en-Provence, 2002).

Brown, R. E., (ed.), *The Gospel According to John*, The Anchor Bible, vol. 29a (London, 1971).

Bruckberger, R.-L., OP, *Mary Magdalene*, translated by H. L. Binsse (London, 1953).

Cassian, J., *The Institutes. The Conferences*, in *Nicene and Post-Nicene Fathers*, Series 2, vol. 11, edited by P. Schaff (Grand Rapids and Edinburgh, 1894).

Cassien, J., *Conférences*, Latin text edited and translated into French with notes by Dom E. Pichéry, Sources Chré-

tiennes, vols 42, 54, 64 (Paris, 1955, 1958, 1959).
Cassien, J., *Institutions cénobitiques*, Latin text edited and translated into French with notes by J.-C. Guy, Sources Chrétiennes, 109 (Paris, 1965).
Christiani, L., *Jean Cassien. La spiritualité du désert* (Caudebec-en-Caux, 1946; reprinted 1991).
Chrysostom, J., *Homilies on the Gospel of John*, in *Nicene and Post-Nicene Fathers*, Series 1, vol. 14, edited by P. Schaff (Grand Rapids and Edinburgh, 1889).
Climacus, J., *The Ladder of Divine Ascent*, translated by Archimandrite L. Moore (London, 1959).
Collins, R., *Early Medieval Spain*, 2nd edition (London, 1995).
Daniélou, J., *Les anges et leur mission (d'après les Pères de l'Église)*, 2nd edition (Chevetogne, 1953).
Daniélou, J., *Jean-Baptiste, témoin de l'Agneau* (Paris, 1964).
Devoucoux du Buysson, P., OP, *La crypte et les sarcophages de la basilique de Saint-Maximin*, Les Cahiers de la Sainte-Baume, No. 13 (La Sainte-Baume, n.d.).
Devoucoux du Buysson, P., OP, *Le guide du pèlerin à la grotte de sainte Marie-Madeleine*, Les Cahiers de la Sainte-Baume, No. 10 (La Sainte-Baume, 1998).
Devoucoux du Buysson, P., OP, *Histoire abgrégée de la Sainte-Baume* (La Sainte-Baume, 1996).
Devoucoux du Buysson, P., OP, *Histoires du pèlerinage à Saint-Maximin et à la Sainte-Baume: Au temps des comtes de Provence 1248–1481* (La Sainte-Baume, 1994).
Devoucoux du Buysson, P., OP, *Jean Cassien, ermite et Provençal*, Les Cahiers de la Sainte-Baume No. 14 (La Sainte-Baume, 2002).
Devoucoux du Buysson, P., OP, *Mais qui est donc Marie-Madeleine*? Trois études exégétiques sur l'Unité de Marie-Madeleine, Les Cahiers de la Sainte-Baume, Nos 1–3 (La Sainte-Baume, n.d.).
Devoucoux du Buysson, P., OP, *Marie-Madeleine à la Sainte-Baume*. Histoire de la tradition, des origines,

jusqu'en 1279, Les Cahiers de la Sainte-Baume, Nos 4–5 (La Sainte-Baume, 1987; reprint, 1998).

Devoucoux du Buysson, P., OP, *Marie-Madeleine repose-t-elle à Saint-Maximin?* Les Cahiers de la Sainte-Baume, No. 6 (La Sainte-Baume, 1989).

Devoucoux du Buysson, P., OP, *Le Père Marie-Etienne Vayssière. Un demi-siècle d'histoire de la Sainte-Baume 1900-1940*, Les Cahiers de la Sainte-Baume, No. 7 (La Sainte-Baume, 1991).

Devoucoux du Buysson, P., OP, *La Sainte Baume: Haut-lieu de la Provence* (Marseilles, 1993).

Devoucoux du Buysson, P., OP, *La tradition de Marie-Madeleine en Provence* (La Sainte-Baume, n.d.).

Devoucoux du Buysson, P., OP, *Vies anciennes de Sainte Marie-Madeleine en Provence*, Les Cahiers de la Sainte-Baume, No. 12 (La Sainte-Baume, n.d.).

Duchesne, L., 'La légende de Sainte Marie-Madeleine', in *Fastes episcopaux de l'Ancienne Gaule*, vol. 1 (Paris, 1894).

Dynamius, P., 'Vita Sancti Marii' (Life of Saint Marius), *Patrologia Latina*, J.-P. Migne, editor, vol. 80, §5540 (Paris, 1844–).

Escudier, J., *L'Évangélisation primitive de la Provence* (Paris, 1913).

Faillon, *M., Monuments inédits sur l'Apostolat de Sainte Marie-Madeleine en Provence*, 2 vols (Paris, 1848).

Feuillet, A., OP, 'Les deux onctions faites sur Jésus, et Marie-Madeleine', in *Revue Thomiste* (juillet–septembre, 1975).

Fixot, M., *La crypte de Saint-Maximin-la-Sainte-Baume* (Aix-en-Provence, 2001).

Garth, H. M., 'Saint Mary Magdalene in Mediaeval Literature', in *Johns Hopkins University Studies in Historical and Political Science*, Series 67, no. 3 (1950).

Gregory of Tours, *Glory of the Martyrs*, translated by R. van Dam (Liverpool, 1988).

Gregory of Tours, *The History of the Franks*, translated and edited by T. Lewis (Harmondsworth, 1974).

Guy, J.-C., *Jean Cassien, Vie et doctrine spirituelle* (Paris, 1961).

Guyon, J., *Les premiers chrétiens en Provence: Guide archéologique* (Paris, 2001).

Guyon, J., Fixot, M. and Carrazé, F., 'Les premiers monuments du culte chrétien à Saint-Maximin. Bilan de deux campagnes de fouilles 1993–1994', in *Bulletin de la Société des Amis du Vieux Toulon et de sa Région*, No. 117 (1995).

Herzfeld, G. (ed. and tr.), *An Old English Martyrology* (London, 1900).

Joinville, J. de, *L'Histoire et chronique du Treschrestien Roy S. Loys IX* (Poitiers, 1547).

Katherine, Sister and Thekla, Sister, *St. Andrew of Crete – The Great Canon with The Life of St. Mary of Egypt* (Whitby, 1974).

Ketter, P., *The Magdalene Question*, translated by H. Koehler (Milwaukee, 1935).

Lacordaire, H.-D., OP, *Sainte Marie-Madeleine*, 3rd edition (Paris, 1872).

Lambert, R., *La Sainte-Baume: Le Pèlerinage des Compagnons du Devoir* (Paris, 1977).

Lauzière, E., OP, *La Basilique de la Madeleine – à Saint-Maximin en Provence*, photographs by H. Daries (Nans les Pins, 2003).

Le Blant, E., *Inscriptions chrétiennes de la Gaule antérieures au VIIIe siècle*, 2 vols (1856–1865).

Le Blant, E., *Les sarcophages chrétiens de la Gaule* (Paris, 1886).

Legault, A., 'An Application of the Form-Critique Method to the Anointings in Galilee and Bethany', in *The Catholic Biblical Quarterly*, vol. 16 (1954).

Mary, Mother and Ware, Archimandrite K. (trs), *The Lenten Triodion*, Service Books of the Orthodox Church (London and Boston, 1978).

Marrou, H., 'Le fondateur de Saint-Victor', in *Provence Historique*, vol. 16 (1966).

Marrou, H., 'Jean Cassien à Marseille', in *Revue du moyen*

âge latin, vol. I.i (1945).

Mérimée, P., *Notes d'un voyage dans le Midi de la France* (Paris, 1835).

Münzer, H., His pilgrimage diary reproduced in Latin in E. Déprez, 'Jérôme Münzer et son voyage dans le Midi de la France en 1494–1495', in *Annales du Midi* (Toulouse, 1936).

Petrarch, F., *Letters of Old Age (Rerum senilium libri I–XVIII)*, translated by A. S. Bernardo, S. Levin and R. A. Bernardo (Baltimore and London, 1992).

Petrarch, F., *The Life of Solitude*, translated by J. Zeitlin (Urbana, IL, 1924).

Ridley, E. (tr.), *The Pharsalia of Lucan* (London, 1896).

Ruffi, A. de, *Histoire de Marseille* (Marseilles, 1642; 2nd enlarged edn, 1696).

Rutebeuf, *La vie de Sainte Marie l'Égyptienne*, translated with an introduction by M.-A. Glomeau (Paris, 1925).

Salimbene da Parma, *The Chronicle of Salimbene de Adam*, translated by J. L. Baird, G. Baglivi and J. R. Kane, Medieval and Renaissance Text Studies, vol. 40 (Binghampton, NY, 1988).

Saxer, V., 'La crypte et les sarcophages de Saint-Maximin dans la littérature latine du Moyen Age', in *Provence historique*, vol. V (1955).

Saxer, V., *Le culte de Marie-Madeleine en Occident des origines à la fin du Moyen Age* (Auxerre-Paris, 1959).

Saxer, V., *Le dossier vézelien de Marie-Madeleine*, Subsidia Hagiographica, No. 57 (Brussels, 1975).

Saxer, V., 'Les origines du culte de Sainte Marie-Madeleine en Occident', in *Marie-Madeleine dans la mystique, les arts et les lettres*, edited by E. Duperray (Paris, 1989).

Saxer, V., 'Les ossements dits de Sainte Marie-Madeleine conservés à Saint-Maximin-la-Sainte-Baume', in *Provence historique*, vol. XXVII (1977).

Sicard, M. M., *Sainte Marie-Madeleine. La tradition et la critique*, 3 vols (Paris, 1910).

Spetsieris, J., *I erimitis Photeini eis tin eremon tou Iordanou*, 6th edition (Volos, 1971). Quoted in *The*

Lenten Triodion, translated by Mother Mary and Archimandrite K. Ware. For an English translation, see J. Spetsieris, *The Hermitess Photini* (Florence, AZ, 2006).

Valatx, *L., La basilique de Saint-Maximin-la-Sainte-Baume* (Toulon, 1927).

Valentin, J., *The Monks of Mount Athos*, translated by D. Athill (London, 1960).

Voragine, J. de, *The Golden Legend or Lives of the Saints*, Englished by William Caxton (1483), Temple Classics, edited by F. S. Ellis (London, 1900).

Voreux, D., *Sainte Marie-Madeleine, quelle est donc cette femme?* (Paris, 1963).

Waltheym, H. von, 'Deux voyageurs allemands en Provence au XVème siècle', in *Provence historique*, vol. 166 (1991).

Ward, B., *Harlots of the Desert* (Oxford, 1987).

Ward, B., *Sayings of the Desert Fathers. The Alphabetical Collection*, 2nd revised edn (London and Oxford, 1981).

Ware, Archimandrite (now Metropolitan) K., 'The Value of the Material Creation', in *Sobornost* 6:3 Summer 1971.

Wyzewa, T. de, *La Legende dorée de Jacques Voragine* (Paris, 1910).

Zander, V., *The Life of Saint Seraphim*, translated by Sister Gabriel Anne (London, 1975).

Zernov, N., *St Sergius – Builder of Russia* (London, 1939).

www.ingramcontent.com/pod-product-compliance
Ingram Content Group UK Ltd.
Pitfield, Milton Keynes, MK11 3LW, UK
UKHW041827200726
13854UKWH00002BA/631